SEASON TO TASTE

SEASON
TO
TASTE
by
Colin Dence OBE

"— and when a broth is too sweet, to sharpen it with
Verjuice, when too tart, to sweeten it with sugar; when flat
and wallowish, to quicken it with oranges and lemons; and
when too bitter to make it pleasant with herbs and spices."
GERVASE MARKHAM
The English Housewife
1631

FOOD TRADE PRESS

Orpington, England, 1985

First Published 1985

© Food Trade Press Ltd
ISBN 0 900379 32 4

Typesetting by
Clavier Phototypesetting Ltd, Southend-on-Sea, Essex

Printed and bound by
The Garden City Press Ltd, Letchworth, Herts.

Author's Acknowledgements

I am grateful to Prof Harry Nursten, of the University of Reading,
for vetting the text, and Mr Alan Fryer, of the University of Leeds,
for translating the Lombard recipes from mediaeval Italian. The
Worshipful Company of Grocers generously allowed me to quote
from their records, and the Brotherton Library, whose collection of
old recipe books must be unrivalled, was of great assistance.

Colin Dence, June 1985.

Contents

Foreword

Part III — THE SEASONING OF FOOD TODAY

APPENDIX   Condiments and seasonings

BIBLIOGRAPHY

SUPPLIERS ADVERTISEMENTS

Foreword

This is the first book ever to be written about the theory and practice of seasoning food. Let me explain how it came to be written. I was trained as a scientist before entering the family food business in which I spent my business life. This kind of training was the best thing that happened to me because it taught me the habit of observing and analysing the nature of food. What really happens when one cooks food; where does the flavour of the food reside, in its taste or in its aroma? I had always been intrigued by these questions but they became all the more important when I started to become interested in food seasonings. My interest was further aroused by a period of service on a government body — the Food Standards Committee, which had the duty of advising the Minister of Food on all aspects of the setting of standards of quality for foods. This proved good training in yet another aspect of food quality. There were still, however, several major blanks in my knowledge of food flavour before I felt fitted to write a book on seasoning, and only retirement from active service in the food industry gave me the leisure which I needed to fill them.

Less than a month after retirement I set off on a tour of the spice growing areas of the world, first the West Indian islands and then across the Pacific to the Spice Islands of Indonesia, in order to see these extraordinary trees and plants growing under their original surroundings. Pepper vines and trees on which grew Cloves, another tree which produced both Mace and Nutmeg, and trees from which the bark was stripped off to provide us with Cinnamon. I came to ask myself why it was that men risked life and limb to sail across the world in small ships to obtain these precious substances to give their food additional flavour. So it was that I came to realise that as soon as I returned I must research back into the literature to find out why and how men and women had seasoned their food in the past. In practice, this involved spending long hours in the British Library and in other libraries, such as the Brotherton Library at Leeds University, ascertaining from old recipe and cookery books the kind of seasonings which had been used in food.

My search was richly rewarded. I found that there was no evidence at all for the oft repeated assertion that spices had mainly been used to mask the flavour of food that had deteriorated owing to the absence of modern means of refrigeration. On the contrary, I found that many old books gave detailed advice as to the correct way of storing food to keep it in sound condition. What I did find was the enormous influence of the church on the use of seasonings, because they were used to give flavour to food during the many periods of the year when the rules of fasting and abstinence forbade the use of meat, and at times, such as Lent, even fish and dairy products. At these times seasonings were used to flavour food which on such occasions would be severely lacking in flavour.

This study into the past also revealed how the methods of cookery in the early days influenced the seasoning of the dishes that were in use. The fact that most meals were cooked in a single clay pot or, in richer households, an iron or a brass cooking pot, meant that all the ingredients had to be cooked in the same cooking pot together; the meat, the fish, the cereals, the vegetables and the fruit were cooked together with any sugar or honey that was available. This mixture of ingredients inevitably produced dishes that were predominantly sweet-sour in nature. Only in the seventeenth century did methods of cookery improve and allowed the different ingredients to be cooked in separate 'sauce' pans on the new iron cooking stoves that started to come into use. This allowed the pudding course to come into existence as a separate course, thus effecting a separation of the sweet and the sour ingredients from the meat and the fish, and allowing the introduction of 'savoury' food.

The book is divided into three parts. The first is a description of the seasonings themselves, those that add aroma to food, and those that affect its taste, such as salt, sugar and the sour seasonings, and meatiness, hotness and bitterness. The interaction of taste and aroma is of fundamental importance to seasoning. The second part is a study of the way in which seasonings were used by our ancestors, and is a description of the research I undertook into the way in which food was seasoned in the past. The third and final part describes a method of seasoning which is suited to the equipment available today.

There are a great number of aromatic seasonings that it is possible to use to add additional aroma to food but no cook can possibly spare the time during the preparation of a meal to add, let us say, half a dozen separate herbs or spices to a dish. The cooks of the past invariably overcame this difficulty by the use of a previously prepared mix of seasonings, such as a spice mix and a herb mix. Mixes of seasonings can be prepared which are suitable for various kinds of dish, and these are fully discussed and described.

Even before a decision has been made to season a dish, it is necessary to decide whether or not the natural flavour of a dish can be improved by seasoning, and it is of no value to add seasonings to a dish which for one reason or another has lost its natural flavour, either perhaps because of overlong storage in a refrigerator, or by reason of carelessness in the handling or cooking of the basic food. There are also cases where cooks have recognised that the basic flavour of the food is so fine that to add seasonings could only mask its fine flavour. Many basic foods, however, have a naturally mild flavour which can be improved and set off by a judicious addition of a seasoning that is harmonious with it.

Lastly, it must be said that this is not just another recipe book, and only sufficient recipes have been included to illustrate a particular type of seasoning. There are, however, a number of specialised foods, such as sauces, pickles and curries, in which seasonings play a major role, and an appendix is included that gives a number of tried and tested recipes, some of which have been formulated by the author.

Part I — *Which are the Seasonings?*

(a) Taste and aroma

Rue, half a leaf or naught, for know that it is strong and bitter.
THE GOODMAN OF PARIS. 1393.

This was the advice given to his young wife by the writer of a remarkable record which has survived from a merchant of 14th century Paris. He obviously knew all about the seasoning of food and, although he may not have possessed our scientific knowledge, he must have realised that we possess two senses by means of which we can detect and appreciate the flavour of food — the sense of taste, and the sense of smell. The taste buds which cover the surface of the tongue can detect saltiness, sweetness, bitterness and pungency; there is some evidence too that meatiness can be detected by the tongue. The gland of smell is situated high up at the back of the nose, and is sensitive to a very wide range of odours, and these are termed aromas when applied to food.

The working of this mechanism can be demonstrated by eating a food which has an aroma and a taste, such as a piece of fruit, whilst pinching the nostrils to stop the flow of air from reaching the smelling gland. At once the aroma of the fruit will disappear, and all that is left will be the taste of the sweetness and sourness of the fruit. As soon as the flow of air is restored, the aroma will reappear. The smelling gland is wonderfully sensitive, and its mechanism has been described by Moncrieff as follows:

"Adsorption of an odour on the gland of smell is a process which involves concentration from three into two dimensions. The molecules of the substance which are floating in the air and occupy three dimensions in space, enter the nose and are then adsorbed on to the sensitive sense cells, and are thus 'concentrated' into two dimensions on the surface of the cells concerned. The strength of the aroma depends on the number of molecules which are adsorbed, and a stage can be reached when all the cells are affected, and then the odour can be said to have saturated them. Once the odour has been removed, the molecules leave the sensitive surface, and pass out with the expired air, until the cells are clear and once again free to receive impressions. This process of adsorption is quite distinct from absorption, that is spelled with a 'b', which is similar to the manner in which a sponge absorbs a liquid and gives it up again when it is squeezed. No process of concentration is involved, as it is in the case of adsorption."

This explains how one aroma can swamp another, and how it is that deodorants can blank out undesirable smells; it also explains why we cannot smell when our nose is blocked up by a cold.

Foods, like meat, fish, vegetables and cereals, all have relatively mild flavours but seasonings differ from them in possessing either tastes or aromas which are too strong to be eaten by themselves. They have to be mixed with the mild tasting foods before their flavour can become acceptable and be appreciated. Their flavour is then combined with that of the mild foods, and it is judged by the picture which is built up in the brain by the two senses of taste and smell. It is necessary, however, to separate the taste from the aroma of a dish in order to judge whether either of them is deficient or possibly too strong.

This combination of taste and aroma, that controls the picture or impression of flavour, which forms in our minds, is a judgement that we make automatically. For example, when we bite an apple we gain an immediate impression of its flavour, and there is no need for us to worry about separating the two constituents of the flavour unless we desire to make a critical appreciation of the flavour of an individual variety of apple. Anyone who desires to season food in an intelligent manner has got to get into the habit of making this taste and aroma judgment deliberately, if only to be able to add a taste or an aroma to a particular dish. The necessity for this will become apparent as we examine the individual seasonings and list the flavour harmonies that can exist between different combinations of seasonings and basic foods. After a time we shall find that we are able to make this assessment of taste and aroma whenever we taste food, and it is an indispensable means of raising our standard of discrimination between foods of different quality. It will then become possible for us to adjust the flavour of our dishes by adding another aroma, perhaps a herb or a spice, or by adjusting the taste by adding sweetness or sourness, if this is necessary.

The quotation I used at the head of this chapter, about the bitterness of Rue, is a reminder that some of the seasonings have very strong tastes or aromas, and we have to be very careful that we do not use too much of those seasonings with the powerful flavours, such as garlic, sage or tarragon. Fortunately, there are many herbs whose flavour is relatively mild, and these we can use with less risk that their flavour may penetrate and mask the main flavour of a dish. Nevertheless, garlic and tarragon, for example, are excellent herbs and it must always be remembered that it is within the power of the cook to use less of them. The matter of 'balance', between different flavours, is a very important one which we shall tackle in the third section of this book.

Always we must remind ourselves that, with certain exceptions, seasonings should only be used to supplement the flavour of a basic food, and it is bad practice to add so much of one of the strong tasting seasonings that we mask the delicate flavour of meat, fish or vegetable. The exceptions are such dishes as curries, where the flavour of the curry seeds is intended to provide the main aroma of the dish. However, a curry has to have a taste as well as an aroma, and this is provided by the meat or other basic food. Another exception is perhaps a stuffing, such as sage and onion stuffing, where these are expected to be prominent over and above other flavours. This matter of the relative strength of different tastes and aromas will sort itself out as the story of seasoning unfolds.

(b) The herb aromas

Vegetables were the main source of nourishment in the early days and, until Victorian times, every home used to have a patch of ground, called a pightle in some parts of the country, where vegetables were grown. These invariably included herbs, some for use in salads, some for salves and medicines, and above all the aromatic herbs to season food. In 1700 a certain Timothy Nourse wrote The Campania Foelix, which contains a list of the herbs that should be grown in the herb garden. He divided his vegetable garden as follows:

"The first quarter of the garden should be planted with the odiferous herbs such as Thyme, Winter Savory, Marjoram of all sorts, Sorrel, Bourglass or Langue de Beef, Borage, Orach, Bloodwort, Comfrey, Spinage, Leeks, Onions, Garlick, Parsley, Hyssop, Staeches, Muscovy, Sweet Moudlin, Southern Wood, Fennel, Baum, Angelica, Lavender, Origany or Pennyroyal, and Beets of all sorts."

The second quarter of the garden was devoted to the root crops, which need not concern us here, while the third quarter was devoted to the Sallet or Salad Herbs.

"Lettuce of all sorts, Chervil, Burnet, Chivet, Endive, Spinage, Alisanders, Sweet Basil, Rampions, Roket, Celery, Sage, Corn Salad, Purslane, Cucumbers, Garden Cress, etc."

Lastly, in the fourth quarter there were planted vegetables like asparagus, brocoli, savoys, beans, and he adds:

"Let there be planted up and down the beds such common flowers as may serve as garniture or show as Columbines, Pinks, Lillies, Star Wort, Flos-Solis, Holy Oaks, Common Carnations, Gilliflowers, etc, as likewise let there be provision made in every quarter for Physic Herbs."

There are obvious errors in his lists, for example Sorrel is not an odiferous herb, and Basil, which is aromatic, is in the wrong list, perhaps the placing of his herbs in the garden was governed by considerations other than whether or not they were aromatic. This list is interesting because Nourse makes a distinction between the different groups of herbs in use in his time. This was the great age of the Sallet, and recipe books of the period gave detailed directions for the making of Sallets of all kinds. There were Simple Sallets, Compound Sallets, which included the 'young knots and buds of all manner of herbs at their first springing, as Red Sage, Mint, Lettuce, Violets, Marigolds', and there were preserved Sallets, pickled and preserved in Vinegar.

At the time when Timothy Nourse was writing, a major change was taking place from the sweet-sour food of mediaeval times to the savoury food of the 18th century. Aromatic herbs, such as the thymes, basil, savory, sage and bay, were coming increasingly into use because they harmonised so well with the new savoury dishes and the sauces which accompanied them.

The Sweet or Aromatic Herbs

At this time, we find a new expression being used by the writers of recipe and cookery books. John Murrell in his New Booke of Cookerie of 1621, said in a recipe for a roast knuckle of Veal, "Take Sorrel, Parsley and a faggote of sweete hearbes". This new appellation is used to an increasing extent in later years but what were these sweet herbs? It was over a hundred years before Hannah Glasse answered this question in her Art of Cookery, published in 1747. In a recipe for roasting a Hare she said "Take some sweet herbs of all sorts, such as Basil, Marjoram, Winter Savory and a little Thyme, chopped very fine".

I use the sweet herbs a great deal, and I have come to recognise that there is a sense in which these herbs possess a 'sweet' taste — not of course the sweetness given by sugar but a sweetness of a different quality. It is always difficult to find words which can adequately describe the flavours of seasonings but, as the vocabulary of the wine tasters shows, it is sometimes possible to find words which convey an impression of a taste or an aroma. Hannah Glasse's list of sweet herbs is clearly not a complete one, and the question arises as to which others could be added to it. The term most generally in use today is Bouquet Garni, and Larousse Gastronomique says of this herb mixture 'It consists of aromatic herbs or plants tied together in a little faggot. The proportion of these plants — Parsley, Thyme and Bayleaf — is adjusted according to the nature of the dish. In the composition of the bouquet, the strength of the Thyme and the Bayleaf must be taken into account, and these aromatics should be used sparingly'. Larousse goes on to say 'for certain kinds of dishes, aromatic bouquets are made containing highly scented plants and herbs, such as Basil, Celery, Chervil, Tarragon, Burnet, Rosemary, Savory, etc.'*

There is great disagreement among the authorities as to which herbs should be used in a bouquet, and the following advice is based on my own experience. First, purchasers have the right to know which ingredients are used in a herb mix, so each package should display this information. The English term Sweet Herbs, and the French one Bouquet Garni, cover broadly the same thing — a mix of certain varieties of aromatic herbs. There is a certain similarity between the sweet herbs in Hannah Glasse's list: thyme, sweet marjoram, sweet basil and winter savory, all of which, while having their

*I would not have regarded all these as highly scented herbs.

own characteristic aromas, nevertheless possess a flavour quality which is similar. This similarity is such that it is difficult to differentiate between say, marjoram and savory, unless guided by the difference in the shape of their leaves. Certain herbs almost exclude themselves from such a category as sweet herbs, because they possess an aroma which is too individualistic. Examples are bay which, although very pleasant, can inadvertently be used to excess, and sage which surely cannot be mistaken for anything else.

Parsley is a special case. It is the most widely used of all herbs, yet its flavour is so different from that of the sweet herbs, that it cannot be mistaken for them. Hannah Glasse seems to have taken the same view, because while she uses it freely, she did not number it among her examples of sweet herbs but specifies it separately.

Some people include onions and shallots in their Bouquet Garni and, while of course there is no law against doing so, I regard them as foods in their own right. I am influenced here by my own definition of what constitutes a seasoning, which is that they are foods of such strength of flavour, that they have to be mixed with foods of mild flavour before they can be eaten with enjoyment.

In each chapter I shall include a recipe to illustrate the use of a particular seasoning, in this case the use of Sweet Herbs in Hannah Glasse's recipe for Force Meat Balls. The recipe is just as it was published in her book, before the days when exact quantities were specified. I advise that later chapters of this book should be read in order to ascertain the quantities of herbs that should be used.

To make Force Meat Balls

Now you are to observe that force meat balls are a great addition to all made dishes, made thus: take half a pound of veal, and half a pound of suet, cut fine, and beat in a marble mortar or wooden bowl; have a few sweet herbs and Parsley shred fine, a little Mace dried and beat fine, a small Nutmeg grated, or half a large one, a little Lemon Peel cut very fine, a little Pepper and salt, the yolks of two eggs; mix all these well together, then roll them into little round balls, and some into little long balls; roll them in flour and fry them brown. If they are for anything of white sauce, put a little water in the saucepan, and when the water boils put them in, and let them boil for a few minutes, but never fry them for white sauce.

The non aromatic or Salad Herbs
Timothy Nourse's list shows the large number of herbs used either

for salads or for general use in cookery rather than for their aromatic qualities. They were much used in fast-day dishes, when no meat and often no fish could be used, so that vegetable dishes were the only alternative. Another reason for their use was that these salad herbs harmonised well with the sweet-sour food of the early days. Beet leaves were much used and chopped finely so that they were dispersed throughout the contents of a dish. I illustrate these herbs by a recipe for a Tansy by the 17th century writer Gervase Markham.

A Tansy

First then for making the best Tansy you shall take a certain number of eggs according to the bigness of your frying pan, and break them into a dish, abating ever the white of every third egg. Then with the spoon, you shall cleanse away the little white chicken knots, which stick unto the yolks; then with a little cream beat them exceedingly together: Then take of green wheat blades, Violet leaves, Strawberry leaves, Spinage and Succory, of each a little quantity, and a few Walnut tree buds; chop and beat these all very well, and strain out the juice, mixing it with a little more cream, put it to the eggs and stir all together; then put in a few crumbs of bread well grated, Cinnamon, Nutmeg and salt; then put some sweet butter into the frying pan, and so soon as it is dissolved or melted, put in the Tansy and fry it brown without browning, and with a dish turn it in the pan as occasion shall serve; then serve it up having good store of sugar strewed upon it, for to put in the sugar before will make it heavy; Some used to put of the herb Tansy into it, but the Walnut tree buds do give the better taste or relish, and therefore when you please for to use the one, do not use the other.

The use of sugar in such a recipe as this was typical of the sweet-sour dishes of this period, and the savoury age had yet to dawn. It is the presence of sugar which favours the use of these non aromatic herbs, and the aromatic herbs were never used in these recipes.

The physical nature of herbs
A herb is mainly the leafy part of the plant, and it is the leaf which contains the flavour principles that control its use. Herbs are high in their content of fibre, and the medical effects of roughage in the diet have been known for centuries. Apicius, the great Roman cook, names one of his dishes Pulmentarium ad Ventrem, which can be translated — vegetables for the belly — for the correction of an

imbalance in the diet which must have been well known in his day.

One physical characteristic of the aromatic herbs is of special importance. They contain an aromatic oil which is also volatile, hence they are called volatile oils, or more often 'essential' oils. They are quite different in their nature from other oils, that do not evaporate, although they dissolve in both fats and oils during cookery, which gives them some protection from evaporation. A drop of a volatile oil, such as Oil of Eucalyptus, will leave no trace of its presence on a piece of paper after a few minutes, whereas a 'fixed' oil, such as that from the Olive, will remain on the paper.

The very fact that the essential oils, which are contained in the leaves of aromatic herbs, are volatile, makes the herbs highly perishable in their nature for, as soon as the leaf is bruised, the essential oil can escape into the atmosphere. I shall devote a separate chapter to the keeping qualities of the seasonings, and all that need be said at this point is that the herbs are more subject to deterioration than the seeds or the spices, because the essential oils can so easily escape from the leaves during storage. It is wise never to keep dried herbs for longer than six months, even if they are stored in well stoppered bottles, as I have found by experience that many of the attractive seasonings in the average kitchen have little or no aroma remaining after this length of time.

The important Culinary Herbs
There are a vast number of herbs which can be used in cookery but there are only relatively few which are of importance in the kitchen. Undoubtedly we owe the great number of them to the fact that so many of them had a medical use in the past and, as there are many people who like to try unusual herbs, there is no real reason why they should not be used. Nevertheless, seasoning history shows that there are only about a dozen which have maintained their place, century after century, in cookery. In the description of these herbs which follows, I shall almost certainly omit somebody's favourite but the important ones must, in the general interest, not be overshadowed by discussion of herbs of lesser culinary importance.

Parsley
First in importance in such a list must be parsley, for it has so many uses, and can be used in such a wide range of dishes. In my experience it is the nearest thing to a general flavour enhancer among the

herbs, for the flavour of almost any dish will be better with parsley than without it. It should always be used in the making of stocks of either meat or fish, and its attractive appearance, when chopped and sprinkled on food, gives it an advantage over many other seasonings. It is not a strong tasting herb, therefore it is difficult for it to be used to excess, and although it can easily be masked by other stronger flavours, it still seems to confer a flavour on a dish in its own right.

Thyme
I think thyme must come next, because it confers a highly individual flavour, even though it is numbered among the sweet herbs. It has got what I call a hard bright flavour, and cooks throughout the ages have warned of its high flavouring power and that it should not be used to excess. There are certain dishes which must include it, for instance an oxtail dish definitely requires its presence. It comes in several varieties, many of them having decorative leaves, but the common thyme with its high flavouring power is the usual one to be used, and is closely followed by Lemon Thyme. This variety as the name implies has an unmistakable flavour of lemon, which is most useful in some dishes. I find difficulty in buying it dried, and grow it in the garden in a spot sheltered from frost as it is more susceptible to damage than is common thyme.

Sweet Basil, Sweet Marjoram and Savory
I shall describe these three herbs under the one heading, to stress the fact that, being sweet herbs, they have a lot in common with each other, while still retaining their individual character. It is wise for the cook to become accustomed to the aroma of each of these valuable herbs, for there are certain dishes in which their individual flavours are absolutely necessary. As illustration, I quote the use of basil in turtle soup, and while this soup may be a little unusual today, it has an unrivalled flavour and the herb provides an essential element in it. Nevertheless the main use of the three herbs is as a mixture under the name of sweet herbs or bouquet garni, when their flavours blend together in such a way that, provided no one of the three is used to excess, no single flavour predominates, and a flower-like aroma is conferred on the dish in which they are used. This balanced flavour is a great asset in a dish, and may well have been responsible for the heavy usage of the sweet herbs in past centuries.

Dealing with each herb individually, basil is the most difficult of the three to grow, for it is native to the Mediterranean and, being an annual, needs some protection in northern climates. Marjoram is also an annual but grows well in the average garden. There is a perennial variety, called Pot Marjoram, but some people think it lacks the sweet flavour of the annual variety. It is the Italian variety of marjoram, called Origano, which is so much used in Italian cookery, and I only mention it here to avoid confusion with sweet marjoram. Savory deserves to be more widely known than it is, for it has an excellent flavour. There are two varieties — the annual one called Summer Savory, and the perennial one called Winter Savory, and the latter has a stronger flavour and is to be preferred because it grows into a small shapely bush which is available to the cook throughout the year.

Bay
Many recipes specify a bay leaf, and this herb confers a flavour which is quite different from the sweet herbs. The cook should become familiar with the aroma it provides, for it is pleasant but can give too powerful a flavour if over-used. Perhaps it is for this reason that the recipes often specify a single bay leaf, and this is probably the only herb whose leaf is of such a size as to provide this useful measure of quantity to be used in a dish.

Mint
There are several varieties of this herb, the commonest being called Bowles Mint, while my own favourite is the round leafed Apple Mint. The mints are herbs of occasional use in the sense that their aromas do not really blend with other seasonings. For this reason they are generally used as what I call 'flavour note' herbs; by this I mean that they are herbs that possess a highly individual aroma, which provides the main and predominating flavour of a dish. One excellent use for the mints is in making a cool summer drink where the leaves provide both aroma and decoration. Mint sauce, where the admixture with vinegar and sugar provides a pleasant sweet-sour accompaniment to lamb or mutton, is of course well known.

Sage, Rosemary and Chives
These three herbs I group together, not because they are similar but because they are all flavour-note herbs, and rather like mint in providing flavours which cannot be confused with any other herb. Sage is an almost compulsory ingredient in stuffings for goose or turkey, and is

a strong tasting herb which imposes its aroma over and above any other. Rosemary seems to have earned a reputation for being excellent with lamb, and these reputations when they have been earned over the years are not lightly to be disregarded. I regard it as a herb of occasional use and quite different from the sweet herbs, and not to be used in conjunction with them. The herb chives is a member of the onion family and so hardly comes within my definition of a seasoning but it is used as such, and is very useful for use in salads or as a garnish with other foods.

Garlic
This is an appropriate place for this herb, which has earned its position as a most useful seasoning ever since Roman times. It is a herb of robust aroma which is often disliked because it is sometimes used too heavily. There is a wonderful Greek recipe called Tarama, which is a combination of cod's roe, parsley and garlic, and when properly made the garlic is not over-used, and demonstrates how useful this herb can be in seasoning. Garlic is yet another example of a herb which has a powerful and individual flavour, and the importance of using such seasonings with due discretion cannot be over-emphasised.

Tarragon
This is the last of the herbs I have selected for mention, and tarragon is another of the herbs of powerful flavour, another flavour note herb in fact. It is, however, rarely used, except as tarragon flavoured vinegar, which is most useful when one requires a herb that favours a sweet-sour background. I always use this vinegar in making a French dressing, which is of course a mixture of oil and vinegar with certain other ingredients for use on a salad. Not everybody likes the aroma of the herb however, and an American humourist, Ogden Nash, puts the matter neatly in a travesty of history:

> There are certain people
> Whom certain herbs
> The good digestion disturbs,
> Henry VIII
> divorced Catherine of Aragon
> Because of her excessive use of Tarragon.

There are some herbs which do not fit into any neat and tidy category, in fact this is the case with all seasonings. The dictionary definition of a herb gives little help in providing nice neat categories which would define precisely what a herb is. Celery is a herb but when it is encouraged to run to seed, this seed has many of the flavouring qualities of celery itself. The same thing happens the other way round, for there are several aromatic seeds, of which coriander, fennel and dill are examples, whose leaves bear somewhat the same flavour as the seeds themselves. The Romans used coriander leaves a great deal in their cookery, and these give a flavour reminiscent of, but different from, coriander seeds themselves. The boundaries between the different classes of vegetable seasoning become even more uncertain in the case of the spice clove. Its leaf carries an excellent aroma of the spice, and we just have to accept that scientists get into these difficulties when they seek to draw hard and fast lines of demarcation between one natural product and another.

Nevertheless, it is useful to regard herbs as different in their nature from seeds or spices, so one just has to accept the fact that seeds, and even spices, can carry essential oil in their leaves, on occasion.

(c) The aromatic seed aromas

"Good Master Mustard Seed, I know your patience well, that same cowardly giant-like Ox-beef hath devoured many a gentleman of your house, I promise you your kindred hath made my eye water 'ere now."
BOTTOM — MIDSUMMER NIGHT'S DREAM

Scientists accept the usefulness of a separate category for the Aromatic Seeds because the seeds secrete the essential oil, which is the source of their flavour, in an entirely different way. It is contained within a hard and horny covering, which gives it excellent protection until it is disrupted by grinding and released for use in seasoning. The seed of a plant naturally contains all the elements which are necessary for the future growth of the plant, and whether man requires the seed for seasoning or as a general food, he has to crush its outer shell to release its protein, its starch or its essential oil, as the case may be.

Not all seeds contain an aromatic oil, and some of them are the chief source of supply of the 'fixed' vegetable oils like palm seed oil, sunflower seed oil and so on. Seeds grow in all climates, as one would expect, but some of them are produced by plants which normally only thrive in hot countries. There are eight in number which find their use in seasoning: mustard, dill, aniseed, caraway, cardamom, coriander, cumin and fenugreek. There are others with special uses, such as

Season to Taste

sesame seed and poppy seed, both of which are used for decoration. To these one must add the seeds from the herbs parsley, celery and fennel, and these are often useful because their flavour approximates to the fresh herb and they can be stored for out of season use.

One of the properties of an essential oil is that it can act as a 'carminative', which is the pharmacological term for a substance which has the power of relaxing the muscles of the stomach. Any essential oil can act in this way but in practice those which are most used for this purpose are the oils of aniseed, dill, caraway and coriander. It is a curious property but the medical use of the seeds for this purpose has been largely superseded by modern drugs, although one can still buy liqueurs which contain quite a high content of volatile oil. It should be realised that any dish with a high content of seasonings, such as a curry, tends to 'repeat' or cause belching, because the sphincters which control the entrance to the stomach are relaxed sufficiently to allow the passage of the volatile contents of the stomach. If a curry seems to take rather a long time to digest, it may not be that it was indigestible but that the volatile oil it contained was acting as a carminative.

A well known carminative product used in some countries is the 'gripe water' used as a mild medicine for babies to relieve their flatulence. The sweetened mixture of such ingredients as tincture of dill in water seems to be most acceptable to them.

I consider that the aromas of the three aromatic seeds dill, aniseed and caraway are somewhat similar in their nature, although there is no difficulty in distinguishing one from another. Each of them is harmonious with sugar, and this is why they used to be made up into 'comfits', those little sugared pills, each containing an aromatic seed in its centre, which used to be handed round after a meal.

One of the most important of the seeds is mustard and, in fact, before the discovery of America and the importation of the capsicums, mustard was the main source of hotness among the seasonings. There are three main varieties of the seed — black, brown and white — each with its own flavour notes. The white variety is the one mostly used by domestic users, and this is hot, but in my view lacks the aroma of the other varieties. Mustard is one of those seasonings which has more than its pungency to recommend it, and merchants might well make the more aromatic varieties available to consumers.

Perhaps the most remarkable aromatic seeds are the group that are responsible for the flavour of curry. Now curry is an example of the interaction between seasonings in which the aromas combine to produce another aroma that is quite different in its quality from that of any of its constituents. Quite as remarkable is the fact there is a plant — *Helichrysm angustifolium* by name — which itself has the aroma of curry, and thus earns for itself the name of the Curry plant. Unlike the odour of a true curry, that of the curry plant does not survive the cooking process. The seeds which are mainly responsible for the aroma of curry are coriander and cumin, and they are mandatory ingredients of the curry formula. There is a great number of formulae for curry powder, which is the ground up mixture of the different seeds, and I shall be content to give the one I use myself, which satisfies my palate:

Coriander	6 parts
Ginger, Mustard, Paprika	2 parts of each
Cumin, Fenugreek, Turmeric	1 part of each

Cumin seed has a powerful aroma, and is generally used in small quantities. Turmeric has little flavour but gives the yellow colour traditional with a curry, and the same applies to paprika, which I use mainly for its colour. It is quite usual to use Cayenne pepper to give added hotness but I find that the ginger and mustard give me all the hotness I require. I use other spices in my mix to give additional flavour but they are strictly speaking not an essential part of the curry formula. It is interesting to note that, on a worldwide basis, curries are by far the largest users of seasonings, for not only are they used in many countries but the curry formula itself calls for quantities of seasonings much greater than those used in other dishes.

Curry must have been known to the Romans, for the recipes of Apicius contain dishes with both coriander and cumin. In the 14th century it must have been known also because the Goodman of Paris used cumin, but without coriander, in a recipe he called Comminée de Poulaille, which was a sweet-sour dish of a type common in his day.

A further matter of importance, before I leave curry, is the advantage of making up your own curry powder and grinding your seeds in order to obtain a powder of the maximum possible freshness. Commercial curry powders are often very good but experience has shown that there is inevitably some loss of flavour during the storage period, which is often as long as several months. The flavour of a curry which is freshly ground is quite outstandingly better than a similar one

Season to Taste

made from a powder which has been stored. Remember that once the hard shell of the aromatic seed has been ruptured, the seed has lost its protective covering and the volatile oil can only too easily escape.

Something must now be said about one of the most useful but little known of the aromatic seeds — cardamom. There are several varieties of it, the most common being *Elettaria cardamomum*, grown in many parts of the world, and a second found in Nepal, *Amomum subulatum*, and both have a highly aromatic spice-like aroma but the Nepalese variety has in addition what I can only describe as the flavour of meat extract, most odd but its true. The most exciting variety of all, however, is grown in and is a native of West Africa, and it possesses the additional virtue of pungency. For this reason it is known as Melegueta pepper — scientific name *Amomum melegueta* — and it used to be imported in such quantities to Europe as to earn for the coast of West Africa the name of The Grain Coast.

In mediaeval times it was known as Grains of Paradise, and was a much valued seasoning but alas it is no longer imported into the UK nor I believe to other countries. I think highly of its flavouring qualities, and it is worth quoting what Redgrave said of it in his 'Spices and Condiments'.

"In Africa the spice is much employed by the natives as a condiment for seasoning food but the culinary use of Grains of Paradise seems almost if not entirely forgotten in Great Britain. This is regretable, for the pungency and pleasing flavour of this spice render it a very palatable seasoning".

The other varieties of cardamom are useful too, for they can be used to add flavour to a number of dishes. Redgrave was not conforming to modern terminology in calling Melegueta pepper a spice, for in fact it is an aromatic seed, although perhaps it does resemble a spice in the quality of its aroma.

(d) The spice aromas

"We found a tree whose leaf had the finest smell of Cloves that I ever met with; it was like a laurel leaf but not so large: but I think it is a species of Laurel"

(THE SPANISH CHRONICLER OF CHRISTOPHER COLUMBUS 1493)

Columbus was sailing westward, in the expectation of reaching the Spice Islands by a new westerly route, and he must have been excited as well as greatly puzzled by his discovery of a spice which resembled clove in its aroma but which also resembled pepper in its appearance. What he had actually discovered was a hitherto unknown spice that he named Pimienta, which was the Spanish word for pepper, and which subsequently became known as Pimento, although it is also and most confusingly known as Allspice. Before I say more about it, we must look at the wider spice scene to fill in some gaps in our knowledge.

There is no doubt about the exotic atmosphere that surrounds the word 'spice'. To look at the spices in the glass bottles in our kitchens, they resemble rather drab coloured, dusty and dessicated pieces of vegetable matter, which is exactly what they are. To smell them however is to understand and appreciate the nature of their aroma. There is something almost tropical in their aroma, and in fact it is interesting to realise that many of the more exotic perfumes also come from the tropical islands, which are the home of the spices. In spite of the fact that the word spice has come to signify the exotic, the sensational and even the scandalous, it is surprising how few people could tell you anything about them — how many spices there are, and how they are used in cookery.

The short reason for this lack of knowledge is that they have fallen into disuse in modern cookery, and the little bottles of spices stand almost unused in our kitchens, gathering dust and gradually losing their flavour. With the exception of pepper, the main use of clove is to flavour an apple pie, and of nutmeg to be grated on a baked custard.

How many spices are there? Originally there were six, which were native to Asia — pepper, clove, nutmeg, mace, cinnamon and ginger. There are also a few minor spices, such as turmeric, the yellow colouring of curries, and galingale, a little like ginger in appearance, and used a great deal in former centuries. After the discovery of America, three more spices were added to the six which grew in the old world, making nine in all. These were pimento, which I have already mentioned, vanilla and the capsicums.

In this list of nine spices, I have omitted the varieties of each spice, such as Long peppers, which have an overtone of ginger, and Cubeb pepper used mainly as a medicine, and cassia which resembles cinnamon. One rather odd result of the differing food standards of some countries is that the US authorities allow cassia to be called cinnamon, whereas most countries accept that cassia has a quite different and rather inferior flavour character to that of cinnamon.

Spices all grow in hot or tropical countries, and usually on islands where they are close to the sea, where they are exposed to a hot sun at one moment and to tropical downpours the next. The main home of the spices of the old world is Indonesia, a huge country in geographical extent, which now includes the Molucca or Spice Islands. When I visited this remote part of the world, it was striking to fly over the jungle covered mountains, with here and there the bright green rice fields and islands surrounded by their coral reefs. It is as if the hot and steamy climate favours the development of these exotic aromas. Much the same climate in Central America favours the growth of the vanilla bean, and the pimento berries, which look at first sight rather like pepper.

Great changes in the distribution and growth of spices have followed the discovery and development of the new world, for spices that grew there have been imported into eastern countries — vanilla and the capsicums are examples. The same thing happened in the reverse direction, for Jamaica became a major supplier of ginger and, after more than one attempt, nutmeg and clove trees were transported to the West Indies, so that Grenada is now the world's largest supplier of mace and nutmeg.

In mediaeval times spices were transported by overland caravan to the west, and for many centuries their actual countries of origin were shrouded in mystery, and became the subject of many legends. Arabia was often regarded as their source because it was the last stopping place of the merchants on their long Asian journey to Europe. Naturally prices were high and remained so until the great navigators of the 15th century discovered the spice islands, and the cargoes they carried back with them caused prices to fall to more reasonable levels. Some idea of price can be obtained from early records, for example the Countess of Leicester in 1265 paid 1s. 6d. for two calves, and 22s. 10d. for two oxen, four sheep and three calves, while she paid 12s. per pound for cloves. Cloves were selling at 9s. per pound in 1695, although ginger, then grown by slave labour, was imported into London at a wholesale value of only 1¾d. per pound.

How widely were spices used?
The earliest Board of Trade records date back to 1695, and an analysis of these shows that 270 tons of pepper and 820 tons of ginger were imported during that year. With pepper at 3d. a pound and ginger at only 1¾d., these quantities do not seem unduly high, particularly as quite a lot of the ginger would have been used for medical purposes.

The quantities of the other spices were much lower with pimento at 34 tons and 6½d. a pound; cinnamon, 8 tons at 8s. 5d. a pound; mace only 3 tons but the price as high as 13s.; and nutmeg, 29 tons and at a price of 6s. 6d. a pound.

At these prices, the average man could never have afforded to use spices, and he would no doubt have had to make do with the herbs growing in his garden. Proof that spices were used sparingly at this time comes from the existence of attractive spice boxes, dating from the 17th century, which were fitted with separate compartments, for about six spices, and often marked with the names of the spices they contained. These were nearly always fitted with a lock, which would have been kept by the housekeeper. I mention these points because the view is often expressed that spices were used in considerable quantity in the past to mask the odour of decaying food, a view which does less than justice to the culinary ability of the cooks employed by our ancestors. The real reason for the use of spices will appear later but we must first get the use of spices into perspective, if we are to appreciate the part they played in the history of cookery.

The chemical composition of the spices
I come now to the chemical composition of the spices. In describing the essential oils, which are common to both the herbs and the aromatic seeds, I correctly attributed the flavour of these seasonings to their content of these essential or volatile oils. Scientific precision requires that I say that both the herbs and the seeds contain another constituent, that is to some extent water soluble, and this is known as an oleoresin, and this constituent as well as the volatile oil is leached out of the seasoning during the process of cooking. Now the spices also contain essential oils and oleoresins but they differ from the first two classes of vegetable seasonings in possessing a third constituent which has a not inconsiderable influence on their flavour.

The third constituent is a naturally occurring chemical, which is characteristic of each spice. Pepper contains piperine, clove contains eugenol, cinnamon contains cinnamic aldehyde, ginger a substance called zingiberene, also sometimes called gingerol, and both mace and nutmeg also contain a chemical called myristin, which incidentally is toxic if taken in massive doses. The chemical names are of importance only to the chemist but what is important to us is that these chemicals are not volatile like the essential oils, and this is why the spices seem to retain their flavour much better than the herbs or the seeds. I have samples of clove and other spices in my possession, which I collected several years ago, and these still seem to retain their aroma.

I must now run through the spices to describe their main features and particularly to say something about the kind of food with which they harmonise. The first must obviously be pepper.

Pepper

This spice has been known since the earliest times. The Roman writer Pliny said of it:

> "It is remarkable that the use of Pepper has come so much into favour, as in the case of some foods their sweet taste has been an attraction, and in others their appearance, but Pepper has nothing to recommend it in either fruit or berry. To think that its only pleasing quality is pungency and that we go all the way to India to get it! Who was the first person to try it on his viands, or in his greed for an appetite was not content merely to be hungry? Both Pepper and Ginger grow wild in their countries but nevertheless are bought by weight like gold or silver."

Pepper grows on a vine, and the berries can be seen, green at first, clustering about a stem rather like a catkin. They turn a dull red when they ripen, and when picked are put aside to dry. Their outer skin then darkens and wrinkles to form the black peppercorns we know so well. White peppercorns are produced by brining the freshly picked black peppers to soften their skins, which are then rubbed off to reveal the white kernels underneath, and these are then dried ready for despatch.

The flavour of the two kinds of pepper differs quite a lot. Black pepper has two distinct flavour notes, the first is the pungency which burns the tongue and irritates the nose, and the second is an aromatic quality which is given by the black outer skin. This can be demonstrated by boiling a few peppercorns in some water and tasting the resultant liquid. You will find that it possesses a delightful flavour. White pepper has greater pungency, no doubt because the removal of the surface layer exposes the pungency from the centre of the berry.

Pepper harmonises with a wide range of foods, in fact the only foods which are better without it are those sweetened with sugar. Sweet-sour foods, however, are in a different category and pepper can improve their flavour. The question whether to use white or black

STT–2

pepper is often decided on the ground of appearance, for when the black variety is ground the black specks, which result, can spoil the appearance of such dishes as white soups or cream sauces. One of the main reasons for having a peppermill on the table is the opportunity this gives for the individual to add the flavour of black pepper to a dish, when it would sometimes not be permissible for the cook to do so. An alternative is to add the black peppercorns and remove them before serving a dish in some suitable way. A good example of the use of pepper as the sole seasoning in a dish is provided by Steak au Poivre:

> Take a Rump Steak and rub it with coarsely ground black pepper. Grill it to your taste under a hot grill.

Clove
Cloves grow on a shapely evergreen tree that reaches a height of 50 to 60 ft. The clove is the flower bud, which is picked after flowering, and the little stems of the flower have what looks like four claws clutching the small round seed we know so well. The French call them Clou de Girofle, Clou meaning nail, for they do indeed resemble an old fashioned square headed nail. The clove tree is native to the Molucca Islands, and the earliest reference to it is Chinese, when a Han Emperor was said to have made his courtiers hold a clove in their mouths when they came into his presence to sweeten their breath.

The cloves when picked are green in colour but quickly turn brown while they dry in the hot sun. In Indonesia, huge quantities of cloves are used in the making of cigarettes, and these give off an intense aroma, which is not unpleasant, when they burn. Some people say that cloves were known in Roman times because Pliny mentions a spice which he called Caryophyllon but I have found no evidence that this was the clove that we know. It was not used by the Roman cook Apicius, and it does not seem to have arrived in Europe until much later.

Clove is used in two quite distinct ways, first it can be used on its own in dishes like boiled ham or in apple pie, when its characteristic odour will pervade the dish. Its major use, however, has always been in combination with other spices, such as mace or nutmeg, and this aspect of its use I shall illustrate in a recipe for a Bechamel sauce, which I have taken from a booklet illustrating the recipes of a Mrs Young, who until recently was responsible for the cooking in a small hotel on the shores of Loch Awe in Scotland.

Bechamel Sauce
Ingredients

½ pint milk	1 Onion stuck with one clove
1 Bayleaf	1 Carrot (sliced)
1 Blade of mace	¾ oz Flour
1 dozen peppercorns	¾ oz Butter

Method

Put the herbs and spices into a pan with the onion, carrot and the milk, cover and leave on low heat to infuse. In another pan melt the butter, add the flour and cook for one to two minutes. Draw off the heat and add the strained milk by degrees, stirring all the time, to avoid lumps. Return to heat and, still stirring, bring to the boil, and allow to boil for a few minutes to thicken.

This recipe also illustrates an excellent method of extracting the flavour of the herbs, spices and vegetables, which are, of course, strained off before adding the milk to the butter flour roux. The pepper, mace and clove combination gives an aroma to the sauce, which is quite unlike any of the three spices tasted individually.

Mace and Nutmeg
These two spices can be considered together because they come from the same evergreen tree which, like clove, is native to the Molucca Islands. In appearance the fruit of the tree resembles an apricot but, when it is ripe, it splits open at the bottom rather in the manner of the English horse chestnut, to reveal a bright scarlet centre. When examined closely the scarlet centre turns out to be tough fronds or 'arils' which are tightly wrapped around a central nut. These arils are the mace and, when they are removed and dried, they slowly change colour from red to yellow to form the stiff 'blades' of mace that we know. With the mace removed, the nut can be broken open to reveal a nutmeg — surely one of nature's most carefully wrapped parcels!

It is impossible to describe the flavour of the mace or the nutmeg in words, and you must taste them to appreciate their unusual flavour. I say unusual because, while mace differs from nutmeg, they have a certain similarity of flavour but both of them are quite unlike anything I have ever tasted. It is fair to say that neither spice is ever used on its own but, having said this, I admit that in recent years it has become the practice to grate some nutmeg on a baked custard. This is rather on a par with a recipe for a cocktail that I found in use in Grenada, and which I give here. It is quite pleasant, although I feel that the presence of nutmeg in the recipe owes more to the fact that the spice grows in Grenada than it does to any particular flavour it bestows on the drink.

A cocktail from Grenada

Lime juice	1 part	Water	5 parts	as a syrup
Angostura Bitters	A few drops	Sugar	2 parts	previously
Lemon	A squeeze in each glass.	Rum	3 parts	prepared.
Nutmeg	A generous sprinkling.			

Serve with ice.

Mace was one of the three spices in the formula of Bechamel sauce, and this is a typical use of mace in combination, although it could equally have been nutmeg, because it is entirely a matter of opinion which spice is used. The important point is that both spices make an important addition to the flavour of a dish, provided that certain conditions are met; one condition is that certain other spices are used as well, and another, the nature of the dish, will appear in due course.

Cinnamon and Cassia

Cinnamon is the bark of a tree *Cinnamomum zeylanicum,* and cassia is the bark of three other species of the same Cinnamomum genus. True cinnamon is native to Ceylon and India and the Seychelles, and has been known since before Roman times. The leaves of the tree do not seem to have any of the taste of cinnamon, although the buds of the tree do have a flavour of the spice, and are sometimes sold for flavouring purposes.

The bark is stripped from the smaller branches of the tree, the outer lining of the bark is removed and the remaining bark curls up as it dries into the 'Quills' of cinnamon that we know. Cassia is treated in the same way. Now cinnamon and cassia are sweet spices, that is to say, they do not harmonise with savoury dishes of meat or fish but with those which contain sugar, and especially with those that are sour, and we shall see the important consequences of this fact as the story of spices unfolds. The name cinnamon is of Greek origin, and in old cookery books it is sometimes called 'Synamone' and in France it is called Cannelle.

Ginger

Ginger is the Rhizome or root of a plant — *Zingiber officinale* — that was native to Asia but which has been introduced with success to other parts of the world. The root is scraped to remove its protective skin and is then dried in the sun to form the cream coloured 'race' or 'hand' of ginger. Like some of the other spices it is quite difficult to grind in the domestic kitchen so it is often sold ground into a fine powder. It is a hot or pungent spice, and this may have favoured its popularity in the days before the capsicums were discovered in America.

Ginger varies in its qualities in different parts of the world, and the Jamaican has a reputation for its aroma while the cheaper African ginger is more pungent. Some gingers are more stringy than others and therefore less suitable for making into the Chinese 'stem' ginger, which used to be packed into attractive china pots. Above all other spices, ginger has a strong affinity for sugar, and it is difficult to think of any food, with which it is used, that is not sweet.

Vanilla
This spice is a bean native to Mexico, by name — *Vanilla planifolia*. It is said that one of the Aztec monarchs used to regale himself during the day with many cups of chocolate flavoured with vanilla. The name comes from the old Spanish 'Vainilla' meaning a pod, sheath or scabbard. It is another sweet spice and huge quantities of it are used in ice cream. It does not concern us very much in this study because it was unknown in Europe, although there is no doubt that, if it had been available, it would certainly have been used in sweet dishes. A method some people use to extract its flavour is to immerse a vanilla pod in a tin of sugar, which is then kept for making cakes and similar products.

Pimento
I have told the story of the discovery of this spice whose scientific name is *Pimenta officinalis*. It is another evergreen tree and the aroma of the berry which it produces is most unusual because it seems to combine the pungency of pepper with the aroma of clove. Now the recognition of aromas is a highly specialised operation, and my familiarity with the flavours of spices in many parts of the world makes it necessary to challenge the oft repeated saying that pimento combines the flavours of cinnamon, nutmeg and clove. It is true that the nature of its flavour is very difficult to define, and no doubt it was because of this that the spice became known as Allspice. So deeply has this name 'allspice' sunk into the public consciousness that there are many

people today who think that in using these berries, they are in fact using a mixture of different spices. This of course is not the case, and I take the view that the misconception is due to the misleading description 'allspice'. I have had to use the name here but pimento is the correct name, which I shall use henceforth.

What is the true flavour of pimento? Just as I oppose the misnaming of the spice, I also oppose the misleading description of its aroma as consisting of cinnamon, nutmeg and clove. Clove I will accept but the other two I believe simply mislead the user into thinking that cinnamon and nutmeg may possibly be present. The ascription of an aroma of cinnamon is all the more incorrect because we have seen that it is a sweet spice, and therefore needs to be used in a sweet or sweet-sour dish. Having said all this, I must in fairness praise the aroma of pimento, and it is no wonder that the Russians and the Poles use enormous quantities of the spice, as I found to my surprise when visiting Jamaica. They use it apparently to flavour the salt fish, of which they are very fond.

My main use of pimento is in making pickles, with which I think it harmonises very well, but I also use it in my own savoury spice mix. Here again we have a spice which would undoubtedly have played an important part in the history of seasoning if it had been known earlier than the 15th century.

The Capsicums
The Royal Botanic Gardens at Kew tell me that most authorities now recognise two main species of capsicum. One is *C. annuum L.*, which includes the wrinkled peppers, cluster peppers, cone or tabasco peppers, sweet peppers and paprika, and the other *C. frutescens L.*, the bird chillies including the cherry capsicums. Peppers are known from burial sites in Peru and were widely spread throughout the New World tropics in pre-Columbian times. It is thought that there was either diffusion from there to Mexico, or an independent origin in the latter centre. Columbus took fruits back to Spain with him from his first voyage to the New World, and the seeds are very easily transported, so that they spread rapidly throughout the tropics, for example three varieties of capsicum were recognised in India as early as 1542.*

Once again we find confusion in the naming of the new spice when

*Tropical Crops by J. W. Purseglove (Longman's 1968).

Season to Taste

it was found in America. Because they were found to be hot to the taste, the Spaniards called them 'Pimiento' in distinction to the name 'Pimienta', which they used for Asian peppers. We thus have the odd situation that the very hot variety of capsicum grown in French Guiana, was made into Cayenne pepper. This is now the name for the very hot and fiery powders which are used all over the world. However, worse is to come, for the mild and beautifully flavoured capsicums, which are the speciality of Spain (and other countries), are themselves called red peppers, or in their green unripened form, green peppers. I am not suggesting that there is any need to rename Cayenne pepper as capsicum pepper. The name has been current for far too long to change it, and indeed it does not mislead anyone, as long as we understand how it came about.

The fondness of humans for hotness or pungency in their food is strange in some ways but it is a fact. It would seem that people who live in hot climates are particularly fond of dishes which contain a higher than normal content of the hot capsicums, and whether or not this is due to the fact that hot tasting foods make them sweat, and the consequent evaporation makes them feel cool, I do not know. It is certainly a fact that the consumption of hot peppers, which originated in America, is enormous in the hot countries of Asia. There is hardly a market stall in any tropical country which does not look the better for the displays of scarlet fruits of the popular capsicums.

Not all the capsicums are hot to the taste, for varieties grown in Europe have little or no pungency; Hungary specialises in the making of Paprika — a dried form of the peppers which is used in making what is almost a national dish — Goulash. Spain too grows mild varieties, and from them comes what I consider to be one of the finest cold soups, Gazpacho. I shall give this recipe as an example of the use of this spice in its mild form, which enables one to demonstrate also a remarkable harmony of flavour between three vegetables — tomatoes, cucumbers and the capsicums. It is a recipe obtained from an experienced hotel chef in Mallorca.

Gazpacho Soup
This is a cold soup for serving in summer, and has to be made with a high speed electric blender to achieve a good emulsion of the vegetable oil.
Ingredients

White breadcrumbs	2 oz	Onion	¾ oz
Tomatoes	6 oz	Vegetable oil*	7 oz

Green and red peppers	1 oz	Vinegar	1 oz
Cucumber	1 oz	Salt	¼ oz
Water	7 oz	*Total weight 26 oz*	

*The oil may seem a little high but do not attempt to reduce it for the soup is very good.

Method

Reduce the tomatoes, peppers, cucumber and onion to a puree by grating or liquidising in a blender. Add the water and breadcrumbs to the pulped vegetables. Add the vinegar and salt and oil, and mix vigorously to emulsify the oil with the other ingredients. The length of time will depend on the efficiency of the blender. Cool and serve. It is an improvement to hold back a little of the tomato and the red peppers, and add them almost at the end of the emulsifying process, as by doing so you retain small pieces of the red vegetables, which float on the surface of the soup and improve its appearance. The technically minded will appreciate that this is a soup in which the vegetable oil is emulsified and thus suspended in the pureed vegetables.

This concludes what I have to say about what may be called the vegetable seasonings — herbs, aromatic seeds and spices. There were twelve herbs, most of which may be considered important, eight aromatic seeds and nine spices. A total of twentynine seasonings, which is more than enough from which to choose, even though quite a number of these, such as tarragon, aniseed and caraway, you will be rather unlikely to use in normal cookery. By considering them separately from the seasonings which are tasted by the tongue, we shall be more likely to appreciate the manner in which the tongue tastes dictate the aromas that we select from among the vegetable seasonings.

(e) The tastes

> Add a good quantity of Vinegar so as it may taste pretty and sharp upon the Cinnamon.
>
> GERVASE MARKHAM 1631

When an experienced wine taster says that a wine lacks 'body', or that it has a good 'nose', he is no doubt trying to convey in the best way that he can the taste and aroma of the wine. Certainly, some wine tasters acquire great experience in the art they practise, although sometimes their verbal descriptions are couched in language that means little or nothing to the average person. There are only two ways in which any food, whether wine or solid food, can be experienced by the senses — by taste and aroma. As a scientist I like to keep my feet firmly on the ground, and it would be better if all tasters were to express their opinions in terms of the two senses of taste and of smell, and to avoid wherever possible woolly terms such as 'body' or 'nose'.

I recognise that there are occasions when one has to use unusual terms to describe a flavour, and I have already done this in talking about the 'sweetness' of flavour possessed by some of the herbs. Even so, nothing that anybody can say, can evade the fundamental fact that we have two senses and these must be the foundation of any words used to describe flavour. How these two senses evolved we do not know but one may assume that they became necessary to man to appreciate the differences between the foods which nature provides.

I can best illustrate the operation of the senses of taste and smell by describing the flavour of the orange. While the fruit still hangs green upon the tree, it is sour to the taste because the process of ripening has not yet converted the fruit acid in the fruit to fruit sugar. As ripening proceeds, the fruit sugar increases to a point where the balance between sweetness and sourness becomes attractive to the taste. Other changes in the metabolism of the fruit cause the fruit to change colour and to develop its aroma, some of which is represented by essential oil of orange.

Exactly the same thing happens with the grape, and the vintner knows exactly when to pick his fruit so that the grapes will be able to provide the quantity of grape sugar needed to provide alcohol by fermentation, while leaving sufficient sweetness and sourness to display the aroma of the grape to its greatest advantage. Fruit is nature's best known example of sweet-sour food, and when fruit is added to a dish in any quantity the sugar and the fruit acid it contains will confer sweet-sour qualities on the dish. Fruit acids are not the only agents to acidify food, for another is vinegar, which is produced from sugar by the action of acetifying bacteria. Such bacteria, once they are introduced into a fruit juice or a solution of starch, produce a vinegar which is the strongest acid normally found in food. There is much more to be said about sweetness and sourness but, before I explore it further, I must look at some of the other tastes we shall experience in seasoning.

(f) Saltiness
People vary in their taste for salt, and the reason may be that some

require more or less for their normal bodily processes. Be that how it may, some prefer to adjust the salt content of their food at the table, and the very existence of the salt cellar shows that this has always been so. All that I need say about salt concerns the several different varieties of it that are, or at least used to be, available. Mrs Charlotte Mason in her book 'The Lady's Assistant', published in 1775, tells of four different kinds. First there was Sea salt, made by evaporating sea water over a fire; then there was Bay salt, made by evaporating it in pits clayed on the inside. Then there was Basket salt, made by boiling away the water of salt springs over the fire, and lastly there was Rock salt, which was dug out of the ground and, when very fine, was called salt-gemme.

Now sea water contains salts of magnesium and other impurities that are harmful to humans but most of these can be precipitated by controlled evaporation and removed, leaving the almost pure sodium chloride. At Maldon, in Essex, a salt is produced from sea water which is claimed to be 99.6 percent pure, with only a trace of impurities. Such a salt has a grain of relatively large size, and this is the reason why many people prefer it. All pure salts obviously taste the same when they are dissolved in water but when a grain of salt touches the tongue, it takes a few moments to dissolve in comparison with a salt of fine grain, thus giving a different taste sensation on the surface of the tongue. I believe that these large grains give a more intense sensation to the taste buds with which they are in contact, although it is difficult to prove such a theory. The fact remains that rock salt or a prepared sea salt seems to have a sharper, saltier taste that many people prefer. Salt does not seem to influence the other seasonings we use in food in the same way as do sweetness and sourness, although sweetness alone seems to inhibit or not be harmonious with salt. Why this should be so we do not know. It is foods such as meat and fish which often seem to require the addition of salt.

(g) Bitterness, Hotness and Meatiness

There is not very much to say about bitterness. Some people like it, the bitterness of hops used in the brewing of beer being an example. Certain bitter substances, of which extracts of Gentian or Quassia are examples, are sometimes called 'stomachics' and are said to stimulate the appetite and induce the flow of gastric juices. There are a number of aperitifs on the market, such as Angostura Bitters, which some find attractive to the taste.

Hotness or pungency is different in appealing to a great many

Season to Taste

people, especially in hot countries. For reasons that we do not understand, sweetness does not harmonise with hotness or bitterness, and in this they resemble or are similar to saltiness. Meatiness on the other hand harmonises well with sweetness, always providing that sourness is present. The whole subject of taste requires a lot more research, and perhaps one day we shall have a better understanding of the rather complex taste relationships between one taste and another. It may be that, in terms of the immense length of time during which the human taste mechanism has evolved, fruit has been an essential part of human diet for so long that sweetness and sourness has become a fundamental element in human taste. Perhaps hotness and meatiness came much later in time than the sensations associated with the eating of fruit.

(h) Sweetness and sourness

The research into the food eaten by our ancestors, which I describe in the next part of this book, paid unexpected dividends in regard to their use of sweet and sour food. By studying the old recipe books, I noticed that they often used mixtures of ingredients which are strange to modern eyes. Meat, fish, eggs, raisins, currants and quite often sugar, and in fair quantity judging from the often used instruction 'take good store of sugar'.

It would have been easier to understand the recipes if there had been more specific directions but it was not until the 17th century that specific instructions started to appear. One most revealing instruction was the one I used at the head of this section, and this shows us how important is the presence of sourness to the proper development of the taste of cinnamon. Another and even more important piece of advice, by the same author, Gervase Markham, I used as the quotation on the frontispiece of this book. You will recall what he said:

"When a broth is too sweet, you can sharpen it with Verjuice, when too tart, you can sweeten it with sugar".

Verjuice was a kind of fruit vinegar made from Crab apples in England, and from sour grapes on the continent, it had a good aroma and its sourness was necessary to offset the prevailing sweetness of many of the dishes in mediaeval times.

The key to the understanding of mediaeval cookery is that almost all the recipes were sweet-sour in their nature, for reasons that I shall mention in a moment. It took some time for the realisation to sink in, although I recall the exact moment in the reading room at the British

Library when I was trying to understand why so many of the recipes in 'The Forme of Cury' were so sweet. This manuscript was one of the earliest English examples of a cookery book. I was looking at one particular recipe, which contained both sugar and verjuice, and it occurred to me to look at a number of such recipes to see whether they also contained verjuice or vinegar. Sure enough they did, and when I came to think about it later, I realised that the only way in which dishes containing both meat and sugar could be palatable was by some sour addition to counterbalance the sweetness.

I have already referred to the fact that the main reason for the existence of sweet-sour food in past ages was the limitation imposed by the cooking facilities, for most of the cooking was done in a clay crock in the ashes of the fire or, in a wealthy household, in an iron or even a brass cooking pot hanging over the fire by a chain. Another equally valid reason was the limited table furniture available. Earthenware plates were not available until a much later time, and although the spoon was known, the fork was not invented until the 18th century, and a diner had only a bowl of wood, perhaps a flat wooden trencher as a plate, a knife and a mazer or cup to hold wine. Almost all the ingredients of a dish went into the cooking pot — meat, fish, raisins, nuts, seasonings and all. Such a mixture automatically produces sweet-sour food, and this type of cooking continued until the kitchen was furnished with enough pots and pans to enable the meat course to be separated from the sweet course, which was in the 17th century.

The other reason which favoured sweet-sour food was the strict rule of fasting and abstinence imposed by the ecclesiastical authorities on certain days and at certain seasons of the year. Sugar and other sweet ingredients were allowed on these occasions, and so favoured the use of this kind of food, as we shall see when we study it in more detail.

Here is a typical recipe for a fast day dish, which I have taken from a 15th century work, The Noble Boke of Cookry, which was written 'for a Prynce or any other estately household'. The nature of the dish is implicit in the title 'Egerdouce of Fish', the name being derived from the French 'Aigre-Douce', meaning 'sour-sweet'.

"Take loaches (a small fresh water fish) or tenches or soles, and smite them in pieces. Fry them in oil. Take half wine, half vinegar and sugar, and make a syrup. Put thereto sliced onions, currants and raisins. Put thereto whole spices, good powders and salt. Mince the fish, putting the stock above and serve."

The "good powders" were sweet spices in pounded white sugar, and this recipe was the normal food to be expected in an Elizabethan or Tudor household on a fast day at this time.

It is important to realise that until the middle of the 17th century only one kind of food was known, and at this time recipes began to be given in two alternative versions; for example, William Rabisha, in 1661, gave a 'Sweet Chicken Pye' which contained sweet and sour ingredients, and immediately followed it with 'A Savoury Chicken Pye' which used a savoury gravy. The word savoury' made its first appearance in this century, and the Oxford Dictionary gives the following definition of it:

'Savoury, used in contradistinction to sweet, as the epithet of articles having a stimulating taste or flavour.'

It occurred to me to look up the derivation of the word as used in the 17th century translation of the Bible, the passage being the one when Esau made his father Isaac 'savoury broth such as his father loved'. A scholar tells me that the Hebrew word would more properly be translated as 'tasty'.

So it was that a word came into use to describe a new kind of food that required a quite different seasoning treatment from the sweet-sour food which had existed ever since the 11th century. One of the results of the crusades was the introduction of sugar into Europe from the Middle East. One recipe which has survived from these early times is the Mincemeat Pie or Tart, which is a mixture of meat, dried fruit and apple with the sweet spices ginger and cinnamon. Alas, in England today this is not a true mincemeat tart because the meat is generally omitted and only suet is used. The US Food and Drug Authority would not allow the sale of such a substandard article, and it would have to be labelled mock mincemeat.

It was not easy to recognise that most mediaeval food was sweet-sour in its nature for although certain of the recipes were described as 'Aigre-douce' or its English equivalent 'Eger-douce' to indicate that they were more than ordinarily sweet-sour, there was nothing to indicate that the majority of recipes were also of this nature. This fact can only be deduced from the presence of sweet or sour ingredients in the recipe concerned. The word savoury was then unknown, neither did it become necessary to have a word to describe dishes which, in scientific language were 'neutral' in their chemical nature.

I have attempted in this book to avoid the use of scientific terms, which may not be understood by the lay reader, but it does become difficult at this point to maintain such a resolve. For the benefit of scientific readers therefore, let me say that by sweet-sour food I mean food with a pH value of 3.5 to 4.5; whereas by neutral or savoury food I mean food with a pH of from about 6 to 7. It is, however, the seasonings that were used which give the surest indication of the nature of the food, because the seasonings suitable for sweet food are as different from those used for savoury food, as these themselves are different from sweet-sour food.

(i) Sweet, sweet-sour and savoury dishes

I have prepared a table to illustrate the harmony between the seasonings and certain types of food. For the sake of simplicity I have only listed the important seasonings, and it is worth studying the table in order to become familiar with what may seem rather an arbitrary list of flavour harmonies between foods and seasonings. There are a number of borderline cases, for example cinnamon might well have been included in the list of sweet foods as well as in the sweet-sour one, and some of the curry seeds might well appear in the savoury list as well as in the sweet-sour one, but these hesitations themselves illustrate that flavour harmonies are often matters of opinion. The main advantage of the list is that it simplifies the choice of seasonings, for once the type of dish is known, this reduces the possible number of seasonings that can be added.

A TABLE OF SEASONING AFFINITY

Sweet dishes	Herbs, Non aromatic herbs such as beet, spinage and other salad herbs. Aromatic Seeds such as aniseed, dill and caraway. Spices such as ginger and vanilla.
Sweet-sour dishes	Herbs, Non aromatic herbs such as in sweet dishes. Aromatic seeds such as aniseed, dill, caraway, cardamom, mustard, coriander and cumin. Spices such as cinnamon, ginger, pepper, clove, nutmeg, mace, pimento and the capsicums.
Savory dishes	Herbs, Aromatic herbs such as thyme, marjoram, savory, basil, bay, sage, etc. Aromatic Seeds such as mustard, coriander and cardamom. Spices such as pepper, clove, mace, nutmeg, pimento and the capsicums.

In some ways it would be easier to define sweet-sour and savoury foods using chemical terms, for all one has to talk about is acid and neutral food. This, however, has its disadvantages, because the truth is that sweet-sour dishes are not strongly acid in the chemical sense, in fact they are very weak acids. There would also be many people who would not understand the chemical term 'neutral'. A chemist too would have to introduce the term 'hydrogen ion concentration' or 'pH', and one would find oneself deeply involved in terms which are not really satisfactory in describing the acidity, or lack of it, in different foods. I have, therefore, continued to use the lay terms — sweet or sweet-sour or savoury as the case may be. In talking about acids, I am conscious that the food acids are almost all organic acids, such as acetic, citric and lactic acids, which are very different from and much weaker than the strong mineral acids. This is an appropriate place to say something about the food acids and the foods in which they occur.

(j) The food acids

Fruit is sour by reason of the range of acids which are characteristic of various foods. There is citric acid, which is present as the name implies in citrus fruits. Malic acid occurs chiefly in apples, tartaric acid in grapes, and so on. The citric acid which lemons contain gives a welcome sharpness to certain foods, and the lemon also conveys an aroma that consists mainly of essential oil of lemon, which is harmonious with a whole range of foods, whether sweet-sour or savoury. A Christmas pudding or cake needs lemon and orange to develop its full flavour, and even savoury dishes benefit from its use as a garnish.

Lemon has always been used to mask the fatty taste in foods, although why it does so is not known. It is probably the acidity rather than the aroma of lemon, because vinegar is equally effective. We must not forget, however, that both the lemon and the orange are themselves natural sweet-sour foods in their own right, which are highly acceptable to man. A certain John Dawson, in his 'Good Housewife's Jewel' of 1587, uses both Crab apples and Barberries to add to his recipes, and he preserved the latter in crocks for use in his dishes throughout the year. Barberries are the yellow and very astringent berries of the Berberis shrub, from which a bright yellow dye was sometimes extracted.

There is one other fruit which should be mentioned for the acidity and the flavour which it brings, and that is the tomato. It originated in the new world and therefore does not appear in the recipe books until a late date, when it is called Tomata and not Tomato. It is said to have come first to Spain and then to other Mediterranean countries whose climate suited its growth, and it now forms an important part of our diet. When it is made into Ketchup, it is seasoned with sweet spices, such as cinnamon, but when the tomato is cooked it tends to turn brown and its flavour is altered. This browning is hastened when it is mixed with other ingredients of a savoury type, and its natural flavour is maintained better in sour food. It is for this reason that it is best served as a separate sauce, and not mixed with savoury food.

(k) Wine

Wine is an excellent seasoning in its own right, for when added to other food it confers a flavour which is highly gratifying to the palate. No one would suggest that the best table wines should be used in seasoning, for the act of adding wine changes its taste, and what we are making use of, is its aroma. It is a fact of experience that wines of only moderate quality produce an excellent flavour in a dish. The type of wine used is of more importance, and naturally a white wine would be used to flavour a white sauce or a cream soup, for the sake of appearance. It is perhaps wise to follow established precedent, for example that king of all soups made from the Turtle was originally flavoured with Port wine and not the Sherry, which is generally used today. In making a Sauce Espagnol, I use Madeira wine to great advantage but I advise a degree of caution in adding too great a variety of seasonings to a dish. If I have added spices to my dish, I choose either herbs or wine to supplement them, but not both, for it is my experience that many a dish is spoilt by adding so many seasonings that no single one of them has a chance to produce its full effect. I will deal more fully with this aspect of seasoning in a later chapter.

Wine, of course, is not a seasoning in the sense of my definition that a seasoning is a food that is too strong to be eaten by itself but it can itself be seasoned, and I shall give the classic example of Hippocras Spiced wine, which uses spices that are suitable for such a sweet-sour food. The recipe is one given by the Goodman of Paris of 1393, of whom more later, and is for his spice powder, of which I use a teaspoonful for a bottle of wine.

Cinnamon	11 grams	Grains of Paradise and	
Ginger	28 grams	Clove mixed	15 grams
Nutmeg	5 grams		

As Grains of Paradise are unlikely to be available, I would suggest substituting cardamom, using about 7.5 grams of this aromatic seed and an equal quantity of clove. The wine I use is a sweet one — a Muscat, and I add the ground spice to the bottle, shaking the bottle each day for about four days and then allowing it to settle for another two days before decanting it into a clean bottle. I use a teaspoonful of the spice mix for each bottle.

(l) Vinegar
The acetifying bacteria, which produce the acetic acid that is vinegar, occur very widely, and the vintner tries to avoid their finding entry into his fermenting wine lest they turn it into wine vinegar. The name vinegar means 'sour wine' and is derived from the French 'vin aigre'. Wine vinegar is often thought to have more aroma than the vinegar that is brewed from malted barley, and indeed while the acetic acid is the same in both, the malt cannot match the wine in its aroma. In the past, recipes often contained the injunction 'take strong vinegar' and this dates from the time when a vinegar could vary widely in its strength. Today vinegar is of standard strength, so that the cook's choice has only to be guided by the aroma required for a particular dish.

I always use a wine vinegar in making a French dressing of oil and vinegar, because I am likely to obtain a better flavour by doing so. When, however, all that I require is a vinegar to acidify a dish, or for pickling a vegetable, which itself has quite a strong flavour, then I am satisfied with malt vinegar. There are occasions, such as in the making of a pickle, when it is a positive advantage not to use vinegar at all but a solution of acetic acid of greater strength than the 8 to 10 per cent of normal vinegar. This enables me to use a wider range of flavour ingredients, while still maintaining an acidity strong enough to provide the necessary keeping quality for my pickle. I shall give my own recipe for such a pickle at the end of this chapter.

(m) Lactic Acid
One particular food acid must receive mention because of its importance in milk and cream. Lactic acid is rarely if ever used as a domestic seasoning except in its naturally occurring form. Yet it is an important acidulant in dairy products. This is, therefore, the place where I can say a word about the flavour of cream, which can be of the greatest importance to those who strive to obtain the maximum degree of flavour from this delectable food.

When you come to think about it, fresh cream tasted on its own has very little flavour, although I admit that some creams taste better than others according to their origin and method of preparation. Now if one adds sugar to cream its flavour is greatly improved, but if you also add a degree of sourness, the flavour is further improved. If you now add to this slightly sweet-sour cream an aroma, such as that of a fruit, then the ultimate in flavour is reached. I have mentioned this matter of the flavour of cream because it is such a good illustration of the order of priority in the addition of seasonings. First the taste must be adjusted, and in this case the sweetness and sourness are involved. Only after that is done may one add the desired aroma. I hardly need to stress the excellence of the flavour of strawberries or raspberries and cream, and it is no accident that this is so, for the fruit contributes its own quota of sweetness and sourness, and the cream brings its own very modest quota of sourness in its lactic acid. Many other fruits are also improved by the addition of cream, and I find that gooseberries can be particularly good, provided that all the criteria of sweetness, sourness and aroma are fully met.

It is not possible to talk of lactic acid without mentioning the food in which it is an important constituent — cheese. However, this is not an account of the flavour of cheese but only of the natural food acid which characterises diary products, whether they be cream, butter or cheese. All that remains for me to say about the sweet-sour taste is better said in the context of the contrast between it and the savoury taste, and we shall now turn to this subject.

(n) The Sweet-sour and the Savoury Taste
Before I started to write this book, I had no idea that I should be writing a paragraph such as this. I knew of course that sweet-sour food existed but, if I thought of it at all, it was of something that one enjoyed at the Chinese restaurant. I knew of savoury food too but what I did not know, until I had done the research into the history of seasoning, was the intimate relationship or rather the precise difference between the two. If I repeat myself here, it is only because of the necessity to stress not only that mediaeval food was almost all sweet-sour but that the coming of savoury food, with all that goes with it, was merely a stage in the development of man's taste from the primitive to the civilised. The very fact that I had not realised the big change in eating habits that occurred in the 17th century, emphasises our almost total ignorance of seasoning history and of seasoning practice. Hitherto, we have treated it as an art to be practised by those

who have acquired skill in it. We shall continue to practise the art but, once we have realised and understood some of the basic facts which underlie the art, we shall be able to build our practice on a much more solid foundation.

I am not suggesting that we should rush to the old recipe books and start making some of the mediaeval recipes. Some will do this of course, and I am in little doubt that we shall find that the best of ancient cookery was very good indeed. What I hope we shall do is to take full account of the fundamental importance of sweetness and sourness in food, and start to experiment in adjusting these two tastes to improve our flavours in both sweet-sour and savoury food. This brings me to one of the curious effects of the change-over, which is the appearance in the 18th and 19th centuries of separate sour sauces, to be served with savoury food. The food manufacturers were quick to jump on the band waggon and supply the sort of sauces which cooks like Eliza Acton used to make, such as Mushroom Ketchup and Fruit sauces preserved in vinegar.

It is sometimes fashionable, in gourmet circles, to decry the habit of pouring some Tomato Ketchup and Worcester Sauce on sausages and chops, or perhaps serving a spoonful or two of pickle or chutney on cold meat. Now I maintain that there is nothing in this habit of which anybody need feel ashamed, for the palate craves for some sweetness and sourness in the food that is lacking in the savoury dishes which are so popular today. If the cook does not serve a sweet-sour sauce with savoury food, why should not the diner turn to the food manufacturer to supply this need? In my view it is perfectly legitimate for a bottle of Tomato Ketchup or Sauce to be on the table, for it must be recognised that savoury food can be appreciated all the more when it is tasted against the background provided either by a fruit such as tomato or by a sip of that supreme sweet-sour food — wine!

Savoury food was an advance on the sweet-sour food of former centuries, inasmuch as it provided an entirely new range of flavours to be experienced. However, to take full advantage of the new flavour experience, it is necessary for the cook to possess the conscious knowledge of just how it differs from sweet-sour food. To complete this important chapter, I shall give the sweet-sour pickle which I have developed in order to take advantage of our fuller appreciation of the subtle difference between the two kinds of food. I have attempted to keep the cost as low as possible without sacrificing the all important aroma.

A Sweet-sour Vegetable Pickle
The nature of the recipe
Vegetables form the main base of this pickle, although some fruit is used for the aroma that it provides. In addition to being relatively cheap, vegetables give a desirable firmness and crunchiness, as well as having an excellent flavour. Aroma is contributed by the gherkins, the mustard and, of course, the spices. I prefer turnip rather than swede for this kind of product, and the proportion of the main vegetables has been fixed with an eye to the flavour balance between them.

To ensure adequate keeping qualities it is necessary to use acetic acid of 33 percent strength rather than vinegar, which has insufficient strength. The reason for this is that the vegetables themselves contain a lot of natural water, and while one regrets not having the aroma of a good vinegar, this is more than compensated for by other ingredients. The method of preparation pays particular attention to the keeping qualities of the pickle and, provided that care is taken in the hygiene and cleanliness of the ingredients, the acidity should be sufficient to ensure adequate keeping quality. One aspect of this matter is that the acid strength must not be lowered by adding water, and it is wise to weigh the saucepan beforehand in order to check that the batch size has not been exceeded.

The seasoning is naturally important, and opportunity has been taken to use a mix of spices suitable for a sweet-sour recipe. I have utilised that used by the Goodman of Paris (see appendix) — this is as follows:

Ginger	20 parts	Cinnamon	4½ parts
Clove	2 parts		

Grind the spices in a blender or pound them in a mortar and keep them in a sealed jar. The quantities I have used are, of course, a matter of personal opinion, and may be increased or decreased to suit individual tastes. Two of the seasonings have been given in grams, as they represent quantities too small to be given in ounces.

Ingredients		*lb*	*oz*
1. Cooking apples	Peeled and cored	1	5
2. Tomato puree	Canned puree of 28% concentration		4
3. Onions	Prepared, raw weight	2	5
4. Garlic	Prepared, raw weight		1

	Ingredient	Description	lb	oz
5.	Sugar	Barbados brown or similar	4	0
6.	Salt			2
7.	Cornflour			$4\frac{1}{2}$
8.	Mustard	Dry weight		2
9.	Carrot	Prepared, raw weight	1	10
10.	Gherkins	bottled in vinegar, drained weight	1	4
11.	Turnip	diced, raw weight	1	10
12.	Sultanas	dry weight		14
13.	Apricots	dry weight		8
14.	Acetic acid	33% concentration		15
15.	Pimento (Allspice)	freshly ground		5 grams
16.	Goodman spice mix	freshly ground		18 grams
17.	Black pepper	freshly ground		To taste

Total weight of ingredients 15 lb 4 oz.

Method

Use a saucepan of a size sufficient to hold the whole batch and make a note of the weight of the empty saucepan.

A. Dice the turnip and carrot on the previous day and place in a plastics bucket. Add the acetic acid and marinate overnight so that they can absorb the acid, stir occasionally.

B. Chop the onion and the gherkin, peel and core and chop the apples and add them to the saucepan. Add also the diced turnip and carrot with the acetic acid, bring to the boil and simmer for about thirty minutes, to cook the vegetables. This cooking will release sufficient water from the vegetables, for additional water must not be added.

C. Strain off the liquor from the process saucepan, allow to cool and place it in an electric blender. Add the raw garlic, cornflour, salt and mustard to the blender and mix to ensure thorough chopping and mixing to a smooth cream. Put aside for use later.

D. Add the sugar and the sultanas and apricots and the tomato to the process saucepan, and also the liquor in which the gherkins were packed, and bring to the boil with constant stirring. Remove saucepan from the heat, and add the contents of the blender, a little at a time, with vigorous stirring. Add the Goodman spice mix, the pimento and the black pepper to taste, return to the boil for five minutes to allow thorough blending of the ingredients.

E. Weigh the saucepan and contents, and add any water lost by evaporation.

F. Using a spoon, fill into jars, which have been previously heated in an oven to 250°F. Affix the caps immediately and invert the filled jars to allow the hot pickle to sterilize the insides of the caps.

Note. It may be wise to divide the spice mix and the pimento into two equal portions, adding one half at a time to check the strength of these seasonings.

Part II — *How were Seasonings used in the Past?*

"A cook they had with them for the nones
To boil the chickens and the Mary-bones,
And Poudre Marchante tart and Galingale.
He could roste and sethe and boil and frye,
Make Mortreux and wel bake a pye . . .
For Blankmanger, that made he with the best . . ."

CHAUCER'S TALES

Mediaeval cookery differed greatly from that of the present day because of the lack of modern saucepans, china dishes, plates, forks and spoons. Spoons were used in the kitchen but not at the table. Imagine the kitchen as having a stout table in the centre, for butchery and food preparation, and a wood fire at one side, in front of which stood irons on which meat and game could be hung for roasting. In the chimney hung a chain with hooks from which an iron or even a brass pot could be suspended over the fire. There were also a number of locally made, rather crude, pottery bowls, which could be put on the fire but these were fragile, and one cookery writer advises a wisp of straw on the floor so the hot crock would not crack when it was placed on the cold stone floor. An oven with a separate fire was provided for baking, although smaller houses were often served by communal ovens. A stone or wooden mortar, in which grains could be crushed or spices pounded, was available.

The table furniture was simple too. It consisted of a wooden cup, called a mazer, for drinking, and a knife for each person, for cutting solid food. Liquid food was served in a bowl which could be raised to the mouth, as can be seen from the pictures of feasts in early times.

Solid food was served on a trencher made either of wood, or was a thick slice of stale bread called trencher bread. This would have absorbed the juices of the food placed upon it, and many a man of good appetite would have eaten the trencher as well, hence the expression 'a good trencherman', used of someone who could eat not only the food but the plate as well!

A number of manuscripts have survived from the earliest times, for man has always treasured his recipes and made certain they were passed on to later generations. The quotation from Chaucer records the names of several dishes popular in his day. Mary Bones were marrow bones, a dish of excellent flavour, which we would do well to revive; Mortrews of Fish consisted of ground up fish of various kinds served with almonds and seasoned with sugar and ginger, and this would have been used for a fish day. Blankmanger was very much the same but made of ground up chicken with rice, seasoned with sugar and ginger as before, and pressed into a mould.

I am not going to use valuable space to describe the cookery of any one period in great detail, because for many reasons I do not think we shall go back to this kind of cookery. I doubt too whether we should take kindly to a surfeit of sweet-sour food when we have savoury food of good quality, to which our palates have become accustomed. I shall concentrate on mentioning only those dishes which illustrate the seasoning of the period. There are some excellent reprints of the early books available, and those who are interested can try their hand at some of the dishes. They must remember, however, that most of the dishes are sweet-sour, and this important fact is most unlikely to be mentioned either in the recipes or by those who have reprinted the recipe books.

(a) Roman Cookery

"Add a little vinegar and reduced wine, taste it – if insipid add more broth, if too salty add more honey and sprinkle with savory."
APICIUS FROM 'DE RE COQUINARIA'

Our story starts in Roman times, owing to the remarkable survival of no less than 490 recipes, said to have been written by the Roman cook Apicius. It would seem that we owe their survival to the careful records kept by the monks in church and monastery, and we are fortunate to have them. They portray a highly sophisticated kind of cookery which used wine, and also the unfermented juice of the grape, but which did not use sugar because it was unknown to the

Romans, their only sweetening agent being honey. There are some notable absentees from the list of spices which we know, for while pepper was much used, neither mace, nutmeg nor clove was used by Apicius, and this must surely be positive evidence that they were not known to him. It seems that they did not appear in Europe until six or seven hundred years later.

The absence of clove puzzled me, particularly because Pliny mentioned 'Cariofilii', which is the Latin for clove, but his description of the spice sounds so unlike clove that I have concluded that he must have been describing something else. Apicius uses several herbs, and was specially fond of lovage, oregano and coriander — the herb coriander as well as the seed. A most interesting fact is that Apicius used and thought very highly of a root called Lazer, which also possessed leaves called Silphium. The lazer plant is unfortunately extinct, so that we do not know what this exceptional flavour was. Apicius says in one of his recipes "If you need Lazer flavour, take some nuts, crush them; they will impart to your dish an admirable flavour, replace the used nuts with a like number of fresh nuts". Another reference makes it clear that the nuts were placed in a glass jar with lazer root, and absorbed its flavour. Alas, we shall never know with certainty just what this flavour was.

The first recipe I shall give is what Apicius calls Patina Quotidiana — An everyday dish. Here is my own modernised version of it, very little different, in fact, from his own:

Patina Quotidiana
Ingredients

Six chicken legs or thighs	1 teaspoon chopped lovage
6 frozen stock cubes*	and the same of oregano
2 teaspoons flour	1 small glass of white wine
½ teaspoon black pepper	4 eggs

Method

Dress the chicken legs and place them in a dish with the six frozen stock cubes and half a teaspoon of ground black pepper. Cook in the oven for 60 minutes at 350°F. Remove the chicken from the leg and tip off the stock into a saucepan.

The Roman Sauce

Thicken the stock with the flour and season the sauce with salt, white wine and the chopped herbs.

*The recipe for frozen stock cubes will be given later.

The Omelette
Break two of the eggs, whisk them and add half the chicken meat folded into the omelette. Turn into a serving dish and add some of the Roman sauce. Repeat with the other two eggs and the remainder of the chicken meat and add to the serving dish with the remainder of the sauce.

Roman cookery as represented by Apicius poses a number of translation problems. Some of the Latin words are quite unknown to us, and others give rise to differing interpretations according to the views of the translators. There is one word 'Liquamen', which Barbara Flower and Elizabeth Rosenbaum*think means a fermented fish sauce, named in certain parts of the text as Garum. The other translator Joseph Vehling** believes it to be meat stock, and if he is right, as I believe he is, the recipes of Apicius would be far higher in quality than if they all contained fish sauce. The problem of achieving a correct translation affects Garum itself, because we do not know precisely what the fish called 'Garus' was. I believe that it may have been the anchovy, which matures in brine and develops its typical red colour and flavour. Many points, such as this, will never be resolved with certainty.

The other recipe I have selected is called Pullum Parthicum — Parthian Chicken, which I take from the Vehling translation. One important ingredient is missing — lazer root, and it features the use of caraway in a sweet-sour sauce, both honey and vinegar being used.

Pullum Pathicum
Ingredients

One chicken quartered	6 cubes of frozen stock
One glass white wine	1 tablespoon vegetable oil
$\frac{1}{2}$ teaspoon of ground white pepper	1 teaspoon of chopped lovage
Very small measure of ground caraway seed	1 spoonful honey (see text)
1 oz wheatflour	
Wine vinegar, as much as required.	

Method
Quarter the chicken and lay the pieces in a casserole dish so that

*Flower and Rosenbaum's 'The Roman Cookery Book.

**Vehling's Cookery and Dining in Imperial Rome.

they are in contact with a marinade liquor made with six cubes of frozen stock, a glass of white wine, the vegetable oil and the seasonings, except the caraway ground in a mortar. Black pepper can be used if the black specks do not matter. Leave overnight then cook and drain off the liquor.

The Sauce

Now the tricky part of balancing the sweetness against the sourness. Take the liquor from the casserole, add water to make it up to half a pint and thicken with the wheatflour. Then add a dessert spoonful of honey until you judge that the sweetness is quite discernible. Then add vinegar a few drops at a time until you judge that the sweetness has been balanced by the sourness. You may add more honey if you think necessary. Now crush the caraway seeds in a mortar and add them literally three or four grains at a time, tasting until you can just discern their presence. Cover the chicken pieces with the sauce and serve.

I have described the seasoning at some length in this case, to illustrate the care with which the seasoning process has to be carried out. Every cook will have his or her own method, and some will use whole black peppers, removing them from the Marinade when their flavour has been absorbed.

(b) The sweet-sour cookery of the Lombards

"Never Lombard ate thee with a sauce such as we will do; we will put thee on a dish with Black Pepper and Onions."

I found this quotation when I was examining an old French document, and I was fired with the determination to ascertain more about the Lombards, for the French writer spoke with obvious awe of their prowess in cookery. I am very glad I did so, for my search had important results.

Very little is known of the primitive cookery of the tribes who lived in Europe in the period between the fall of Rome and the rise of the new civilisation, which began to appear in the 7th and 8th centuries AD. The tribes who became the French nation were the Gallo-Romans, who lived in southern France, and the Frankish Goths, who came from the north and east. Northern Italy on the other hand was invaded by a tribe called the Langobards, the long bearded men, in the 5th century. They had crossed the Alps and conquered and absorbed the tribes who lived in the Lombard plain. They were an industrious people who lived in fortified cities all over the plain and, in spite of inter-city wars, they became very wealthy. They quarrelled with France and in AD 773 they were invaded by Charles I of France, later known as Charlemagne, and he, for a time, united a nation of great influence and power. Thus arose a culture from which modern cookery was to spring.

The Lombards were the successors of the Langobards, and I told their history briefly because it was they, rather than the French, who were I believe the founders of European cookery. They were very much in the forefront of the mind of our greatest dramatist Shakespeare, who wrote several of his plays about the Lombards, such as The Merchant of Venice, Othello, Romeo and Juliet, and so on. Only now that I have become familiar with the Lombard story, have I appreciated why, at Capulet's feast where Romeo met his Juliet, the first servant said to the second servant:

"Good thou, save me a piece of Marchpaine, and as thou lovest me, tell the porter to let in Susan Grindstone and Nell—".

But what was Marchpaine? Why, it was the anglicised version of Massepain, which was itself the Italian or Lombard Marzepane, used by the Lombards as a fast day dish.

The Lombards just have to have a part in our story because it was they who became even more wealthy by the mounting of the crusades in 1100 AD and afterwards. From their ports, such as Venice and Genoa, they exported soldiers with all their equipment to the eastern Mediterranean, and on the return voyage their ships carried silks and satins, tapestries, carpets, spices and — most important from our standpoint — sugar. It was sugar from the sugar cane of the Middle East that was destined to change the face of European cookery, and therefore of seasoning.

It was only in the later stages of my study that I realised that the first printed cookery book was not French or English but Lombard. The very first is called 'De Honesta Voluptate', written by a man called Platina, a historian who was employed at one time at the Vatican as a librarian. It was published in 1474 at Ferrara and was in mediaeval Italian. Then I found other similar books of Lombard cookery, also in Italian, and it is no credit to English cookery history that not one of them seems to have been translated into English. I am indebted to a scholar at Leeds University for the translations of the recipes I have studied.

The chief characteristic of Lombard cookery is that it is sweet-sour

Season to Taste

in nature, and makes frequent use of sugar, ginger and cinnamon, to which are often added clove and nutmeg. The recipes often provide for alternative ingredients to be used on fast days and in Lent. In one of them, we are instructed to omit the goat's cheese and substitute for it almond milk and olive oil. There is also great emphasis on the Crustade or tart, for it appears that the Italian expertise on cereal cookery goes right back to Lombard times. I even found a mediaeval recipe for a pizza pie in one of the earliest books.

One of the most famous dishes was the Lombard tart, and I am going to give the recipe for it just as it appears in C de Messisbugo's Banchetti Compositione di Vivandi, published in Ferrara in 1549. I do not feel sufficiently competent in cereal cookery to modernise it myself but I will give the notes from Alan Fryer, to whom I am indebted for the translation. They illustrate how difficult such a translation can be. You will see that it is a cheese, butter and chopped herb mixture cooked in a pastry case. The herbs were chopped beet leaves, which were much used in this kind of cookery, and must have looked very attractive against the background of the golden cheese-butter mix. The question which arises is whether or not to add the sugar and the spices ginger and cinnamon, because this was sweet-sour cookery, yet the recipe itself gives permission for the ginger, cinnamon and the sugar to be omitted. This must, however, be read in the light of the variation in the practice of fasting and abstinence at different times and in different places; and we shall see, as we proceed, that the spices and the sugar would have been added when local practice required the omission of a major ingredient, such as cheese. Here is the recipe:

Torta Lombarda

Take a good handful of Beet leaves,* wash well and shred finely and place in a vessel with two pounds of fresh butter, six eggs and a quarter of ground Pepper (I am sure a quarter of an ounce is meant), also a pinch of Ginger and Cinnamon and half a pound of sugar, if desired, as usually these latter are not added. Then make two pastry cases. Knead the filling well and grease a cake pan with two ounces** of fresh butter and put into the pan one case, then on to that the filling, and then on to the other case, and place the ring***

*These are beet leaves, and really come under the heading of Pot Herbs.
**The measure referred to is the oncia, which is the ounce, but it varied a lot from place to place but was generally the same as the English ounce.
***Ring means literally a 'roll' of some material and suggests a kind of cake ring made of tin.

around it. On top put four ounces of fresh melted butter, and then cook in the oven, or in a pan,**** and when it is almost cooked sprinkle over it three or four ounces of sugar and finish cooking.

Here are Alan Fryer's notes, which I give because they may suggest alternatives to interested cooks.

If any sugar is used, then some counterbalancing acidity must be provided, and quite often such an addition is taken for granted. It is recorded that the Lombard tarts were sold in the streets of Paris in the 14th century, and Pisan tarts too but, in this case, they contained small birds in addition to the other ingredients.

Lombard cookery left many legacies to both English and French cookery, not the least important being the fast day product Marzipan. Another legacy was Lombard or Lumbarde Powder, which was a mixture of spices mixed with beaten sugar but, as these mixtures were often the secret of their makers, they were seldom published. I take a recipe from the Goodman of Paris, whose work we shall see later:

Ginger	20 parts	Cinnamon	$4\frac{1}{2}$ parts
Clove and Grains of		Sugar	73 parts
Paradise (mixed)	$2\frac{1}{4}$ parts		

No doubt such a mixture would have been diluted with even more sugar on occasions, and its presence would have given it a white colour, which would explain the name by which it was often known, Blanche or in England Blank Powder. A different mix was used for making the spice powder used in Hippocras spiced wine.

Fast day Food

One of the features of Lombard cookery, which we meet for the first time, and which is repeated in other cookery cultures, is the paramount influence of the church in the food and diet of the people, and it is this which has had a big influence on the seasoning of food. It could be said that while kings governed the affairs of the state, it was the church which looked after the souls of the people, and part of their method of doing this was to lay down a complex system of fasting and abstinence. It was abstinence from certain foods, rather than fasting, which was the controlling feature, and it was the former rather than the latter which influenced cookery. Until I had studied early recipe books, I had not realised how deeply it affected food habits. In the Greek and other Eastern churches it is said that no less

****Pan is literally 'under an earthenware lid or cover.'

Season to Taste

than 150 days in each year were affected by abstinence in one form or another. The practice was always under the control of individual churches and even dioceses varied in their method of controlling abstinence. It is recorded, for example, that on one day in the week, it was possible to eat meat in coffee houses on one side of Cheapside, in London, whereas on the other side of the street it was banned because it was in a parish controlled by an adjoining diocese.

It was, however, the actual type of abstinence which had most influence on food, and the Eastern Church, on fast days, banned the use not only of meat but also of fish, eggs, milk, cheese, animal fat and even wine. Socrates Scholasticus, who lived in Constantinople, wrote of Christian practice in Lent:

'Some abstain from all kind of living creatures, others from all but fish; others eat fowls as well as fish, saying that, according to Moses, they come out of the water; others abstain from fruit and eggs; others eat only dry bread, and others not even so much as that.'

At certain times, when all the normal protein foods were barred, the only protein available was provided by nuts and, when cow's milk could not be used, almond milk was made by crushing almonds and steeping them in water overnight, to extract the milky fluid that these nuts provided. I have sometimes wondered how the Lombards knew that nuts provided a vital source of protein — I realise, of course, that protein was not heard of in those days. Perhaps experience taught them that nuts were a viable alternative to meat and fish.

Now nuts are harmonious with sugar, and the church allowed the Lombards to use both of them, so is it any wonder that Marzipan was invented and used as a fast day dish? I think it can now be appreciated that the advent of sugar, allied to the banning of many staple foods by edict of the church, put the emphasis heavily on sweet foods, and these favoured the use of the sweet seasonings, such as ginger and cinnamon. We shall see this at work in 14th century Paris, and in fact in the comparable English cookery.

The eminent poet Dante, who was on an embassy from his state to the neighbouring republic of Venice, attended a banquet given by the Doge of that city. It was a fast day, and a fish was served to each of the guests, some of more account than he received much larger fishes than he. This treatment nettled Dante, who took up his fish in his hand and held it to his ear, as though expecting it to say something.

The Doge, observing his action, asked what he meant by this, to which Dante replied "As I knew that the father of this fish met his death in these waters, I was asking him news of his father". "Well," said the Doge "What did he answer?" To which Dante replied "He told me that he and his companions were too young to remember much about him; but that I might learn what I wanted from the older fish, who would be able to give me the news I asked for". Thereupon, the Doge at once ordered him to be served with a fine large fish.

The Doge of Venice would not have been surprised at Dante's action in picking up the fish in his hand, for this was the normal method of eating food. It does however illustrate the table manners of the time before the invention of the fork, when the diners would have used their hands to feed themselves, and they would have been supplied with bowls of rose water and with napkins with which to wipe their hands during the course of a meal.

I could equally well have illustrated the food and eating habits of the time from the records of other nations but it seems to me that the Italian scene has priority, for a number of reasons. Probably many of our finest works of art owe their origin to the Italian Renaissance, and can it be any real surprise that cookery too shared with other arts the glory of that time?

I want now to give a recipe for Marzepane (The Lombard spelling), which again comes from C. de Messisbugo's book. As with the other recipe, I shall give Alan Fryer's translation verbatim:

A Fare dieci piati de Tegole di Pasta di Marzepane
(To make ten plates of Marzepane pods like Beans)[1]
First make two pastry cases as for guanti.[2] Then take one and a half pounds of peeled[3] and ground Ambrosian almonds and half a pound of sugar and mix together with a little Rose water. Spread this (mixture) on the paste, in small dice, each a little larger than the last, like beans in pods.[1] Then turn over the paste and cut it (into) long and thin (pieces) with a knife,[4] like bean pods when they are ripe. Then with your hands press them together so as to make them resemble as much as possible the said (pods). Then fry them very carefully, so as to prevent them breaking, in three pounds of butter or fresh suet. When they are cooked sprinkle over them six ounces of sugar before serving.

Here are Alan Fryer's notes on some of the words:

1. ie, shaped like bean pods.
2. Florio- (Queen Anna's New world of words, 1611) 'a kind of paste meat fashioned as hands'
3. The values of Libra and Oncia varied greatly from region to region. In general 12 oncia = 1 Libra.
4. Florio- 'a brazen toole with a spoone at one end and a trowell at the other, which cooks call a jagging iron'.

His comment under 2. is suggestive because in 14th century Paris we find mention of 'Manus Christi' and I have been unable to ascertain exactly what this was. It may have been Marzipan fashioned in the form of hands but the religious significance of this eludes me. Rose water by the way was always used in a Marzepane recipe and, while not specified by Messisbugo, cinnamon and ginger were added by some cooks.

Finally, may I comment that I deplore the modern habit of calling Marzipan 'almond paste'. It is not, for there is a choice of the original Marzepane, which is Italian, or Massepain-French, or Marchpaine — English — choose which you like!*

*Some workers in this field have suggested that at least some of the recipes used by the Lombards were of Middle Eastern origin, and this may indeed be the case, for if sugar was imported from these areas there is every likelihood that recipes that used sugar may well have been imported as well. A great deal of research still needs to be done into the original sources of Lombard cookery.

(c) The sweet-sour cookery of the French

"Boil for as long as you can say a Miserere"

We are exceedingly well informed about the cookery and the seasoning of 14th century Paris, thanks to a detailed account of it written about the year 1393 by a man who has become known as 'Le Menagier de Paris', which can be roughly translated as The Goodman of Paris. It is addressed to his young wife, whom he had married rather late in life, and tells in graphic language just how he wished her to run his house, supervise his kitchen and entertain his guests. It is an unusual record because, while he was a wealthy merchant, he clearly knew everything to do with the running of a kitchen, and his cook must have had a healthy respect for his encyclopaedic knowledge of the buying, cooking and serving of food. He was what we should today call a gourmet. His descriptions of fast day cookery are of special interest because he is the one man at this early time to give precise instructions to his young wife, when to use, and when not to use seasonings. His manuscript was translated into English from the mediaeval French by Eileen Power, and published in 1928.

This is an example of his advice concerning a spice mix called Cameline, not to be confused with the herb of that name — Camelina Sativa.

"Note that at Tournai to make Cameline they bray (pound) Ginger, Cinnamon, and Saffron and half a Nutmeg moistened with Wine, then take it out of the mortar, then have white breadcrumbs, not toasted but moistened with cold water and brayed in the mortar, moisten them with wine and strain them, then boil all together and put in brown sugar last of all; and that is winter Cameline. And in truth, to my taste, the winter sort is good, but in summer that which followeth is far better; bray a little Ginger and a great deal of Cinnamon, then take it out and have toasted bread moistened, or plenty of bread raspings in vinegar, brayed and strained".

This is typical of the style of his manuscript but he does not say why it was customary to use breadcrumbs in winter, and toast in summer.

One cannot read the Goodman's narrative without realising how much of the food served depended on the church's rules on abstinence, which at this time seem to have been quite strictly observed. This is well illustrated in the following recipe for leeks.

"There be three sorts of porray, according to the saying of cooks, who call them white, green and black. White Porray is so called because it is made of the white of Leeks, chines, chitterlings and ham, in the autumn and winter seasons on meat days; and know that no other fat than pig's fat is good therewith. And first you pick over wash, slice and blanch the leeks, to wit in summer when they be young; but in winter when the aforesaid leeks be older and harder, it behoves you to parboil them, instead of blanching them, and if it be a fish day, after what has been said, you must put them in a pot of hot water and so boil them, and also boil sliced onions and fry the onions, and afterwards fry the leeks with the onions; then put all to cook in a pot of cow's milk, if it be out of Lent and on a fish day; and if it be in Lent one puts Milk of Almonds therein."

Do you see how it was? On a meat day Porray was a meat-based dish, on a fish day cow's milk replaced the ham but in Lent even that was not allowed and almond milk had to be used.

Now nobody could describe this Lenten food as very interesting and, as herbs and spices were allowed to be used on fast days, they were available to provide some flavour, as this recipe for cooking peas

Season to Taste

clearly shows:

> "As to new peas, sometimes they be cooked with sewe (stock) of meat and brayed Parsley to make a green potage and that is for a meat day; and on a fish day they be cooked in milk with Ginger and Saffron therein."

The Goodman does not mention it here but the spiced dish would have had sugar in it almost as a matter of course, and a touch of vinegar as well if cinnamon was used in the dish.

There are one or two more things to be said about the Goodman's seasoning. He uses cumin quite a lot, and here is a recipe for Comminée de Poulaille:

> Cut the Chicken in pieces and put it to cook in water and a little wine, then fry it in fat; then take a little bread dipped in your broth and take first Ginger and Cumin, moisten with Verjuice, bray and strain them and put all together with meat or chicken broth, and then colour it either with saffron or with eggs or yolks run through a strainer and dropped slowly into the pottage after it is taken off the fire. Item, best it is to make it with milk, as aforesaid, and then to bray your bread after your spices, but behoveth it to boil the milk first lest it burn, and after the pottage is finished let the milk be put into wine (meseemeth this is not needful) and fry it. Many there be that fry it not, nathless it tastes best so.

He gives a list of spices to be obtained from the grocer for a feast, and this gives as good an idea as any of just which spices were used. The grocer was called the Epicerie, derived of course from the word for spice — 'epice'.

Columbine ginger	1 lb
Cinnamon	$\frac{1}{2}$ lb
Saffron	1 oz
Clove and Grains of Paradise mixed	$\frac{1}{4}$ lb
Long pepper, galingale, mace, bay leaves each	2 oz
Hippocras Spiced wine	3 quarts

Clove and Grains of Paradise were sold mixed together, and you will recall that the latter is the variety of cardamom which used to be imported from West Africa. Here is the recipe for Hippocras, which he uses, although in the list given above it would seem it was also available from the epicerie; I have modernised it and use it myself. The wine you use is important, and I have found a sweet Muscat to be quite suitable.

Hippocras Spice Powder

Cinnamon	11 grams	Nutmeg	5 grams
Ginger	28 grams	Grains of Paradise	15 grams

As Grains are not likely to be available, I suggest substituting a mixture of $7\frac{1}{2}$ grams each of Cardamom and Clove.

Method

Take a heaped teaspoonful of the Spice Powder (about 7 grams) and add it to the wine in the bottle by means of a funnel. Replace the cork and shake the bottle well until the spices are well dispersed. Allow the wine to stand for two or three days, shaking the bottle each day, then allow it to stand for a week until it has clarified, before decanting it into a clean bottle. Experience will dictate the precise quantity of spice mix to add. Many people will heat the wine and the spices together and filter them off afterwards but I have found my method preferable.

Coarse fish is rarely eaten today because of its relatively poor flavour compared with fish from the sea but, in former times, it had to be eaten whenever the rules of fasting and abstinence required abstention from meat. The monks all had their own fishponds to supply their needs, and the lack of flavour in the fish was remedied by the addition of spices, as is shown in the Goodman's recipe for Carpe a L'Estouffee. The recipe is just as he gave it.

Carpe L'Estouffée

First put minced onions in a pot to boil with water, and when the onions be well cooked, cast in the head and tail, and soon afterwards the pieces of the body and cover it well so that no steam cometh forth. When it is cooked have ready your seasoning of Ginger, Cinnamon and Saffron, moistened with wine and a little Verjuice, to wit the third part (he means I think the pieces of the body only, the head and the tail having contributed their flavour and been removed from the dish) and set all to boil together well covered up; and then serve forth in bowls.

I have used this recipe not because it was a particularly good one but just because it was such an ordinary dish, and typical fare for a fish day. As is often the case, the recipe is not quite complete because of the absence of sugar but it would inevitably have been used in such a

Season to Taste

dish, and this we know from other similar recipes of the period. The flavour would not have been too bad, for the fish and the fish stock would have provided the main taste, while the aroma would have come from the spices set in a sweet-sour background.

One of the lessons we can learn from this sweet-sour cookery is how attractive to the taste it can be, provided that the sweetness and sourness are carefully balanced. I shall not say more about it here, because I shall be devoting a section to it in the third part of this book. The balancing of one flavour against another is of fundamental importance to achieving good flavour in a dish, and there is no question of Carpe Estouffée being a dull dish, if it has been properly seasoned.

The other recipe of the Goodman's, which I am going to give, is one in which he says any meat can be used. I made this up for my own use using chicken as the meat of my choice, and I have named it Poulaille de Menagier, in honour of the first man in European cookery history who took the trouble to write down his cookery experience. I hope that one day his manuscript can be reprinted for the benefit of a public who, I feel sure, would find it most entertaining and enjoyable.

Poulaille de Menagier
This dish consists of cooked chicken in a sweet-sour sauce typical of the period and, for simplicity, I have used chicken legs or thighs which have been grilled. Any other method of cookery can be used but in this recipe I leave the choice to the individual cook, and have concentrated on the preparation of the sauce.
Preparation
1. For two or three people take four chicken legs or thighs, grill them and place them in a suitable serving dish to which the sauce can be added.
2. Prepare a fine spice mix to the Goodman's recipe as follows:
   'Take of Ginger an ounce, of Cinnamon a quarter of an ounce, Clove a quarter of an ounce, Cardamom a quarter of an ounce, and of Sugar a quarter of a pound, and reduce them to a powder in a mortar'.
3. Toast three or four pieces of white bread and moisten them with a wineglassful of white wine. Reduce in a blender.
4. Prepare a meat stock or, if frozen cubes are used, use six stock cubes.
5. Place the chicken giblets and necks, if available, in a saucepan, and cover with water and simmer for an hour. Strain off the stock.

6. Mix the chicken stock, frozen stock cubes and the breadcrumbs, and adjust the thickness of the sauce by adding water or more breadcrumbs as required.

7. Now add a small spoonful of the Goodman's Spice powder, and taste — this is where seasoning skill comes in — first the dish must be slightly sweet — then add a little wine vinegar from a spoon, a little at a time — has the sourness balanced the sweetness? — you can now add either more sugar or more vinegar as judged necessary — can you taste the spices? — add more if you consider you cannot taste them. I suggest that you study the later section on flavour balance before you undertake this operation.

8. Finally heat the sauce and serve with the grilled chicken.

(d) The sweet-sour cookery of the English

"Pike and Eels in Ballok Broth, that must our Dame have or else she will be wroth"

from THE NOBLE BOKE OF COOKRY

While the Goodman was entertaining his friends in Paris with sweet-sour food seasoned with spices, food of a very similar kind was being served in England. This was not very surprising, for the Normans, after their successful invasion in 1066, had brought with them their cookery, and it was practised in castles and homes, in monasteries and nunneries. This is evident in the French and occasional Lombard names in the lists of recipes at which we will now look.

There is a choice of several books from which we can study the seasoning. Unlike the wonderful manuscript left by the Goodman of Paris, we have lists of recipes such as those in the Harleian MS (manuscript) 279 of about 1430, or MS 4016 of about 1450. The MS, which I prefer, is one with the title 'The Noble Boke of Cookry', which is subtitled 'For a Prynce or any other estately household', and I like it because it is written in a rather more chatty style with greater attention to the method of preparation. At any rate, until recently, the MS was in the library of the Earl of Leicester at Holkham, in Norfolk.

Then there was a well known manuscript called the 'Forme of Cury', said to have been a list of all the dishes used by the French cooks employed by Richard II. This is printed in a book called 'Antiquitatis Culinariae', published in 1791 by the Rev Richard Warner. It is clear from his comments on the recipes that he quite failed to grasp the nature of mediaeval food, as can be seen from the rather sarcastic remarks he made about it.

Season to Taste

"In the time of Richard II the prodigality of entertainments rose to its greatest heights. In his time the French cooks were in fashion and in the variety of their condiments and in their faculty of disguising nature and changing simple food into complex and nondescript Gillimawfries, they were experts. Such were the recipes in 'The Forme of Cury', which are indeed as unintelligible as the heiroglyphics on an Egyptian pillar; but such as we do understand are not calculated to prejudice as much in favour of the culinary art of the 14th century."

Now this talk of Gillimawfries is most unfair to the cooks of Richard II who were the best of their day. Of course the elaborate dishes, moulded in the shape of abbeys and castles, and dressed in all the colours of heraldry, were constructed simply to pay honour to the King's banquets in Westminster Hall; but these were merely the trappings of royal occasions, which were thought worthy of record by reason of their very singularity and splendour. Ordinary recipes were described as well, as we shall see in due course.

The truth of the matter is that Richard Warner had quite failed to appreciate that most of the recipes were sweet-sour in their nature, because savoury cooking had not then been invented, and could not have existed with the primitive cooking pots of the early days. He was used to the new savoury cooking, and already the cookery of the sixteenth century had faded from memory.

In one recipe for Pessen Ryalle, we are told, as a guide to recipe quantities, that a pot of four gallons would require twelve raw eggs to thicken the stew of peas and other ingredients. Now four gallons weighs about forty pounds, and shows the sort of scale of the cookery in a mediaeval household, feeding both the family and its retainers with a cheap and nourishing meal of stewed peas with a capon in it, always providing of course that it was a meat day. The great majority of the dishes were sweet-sour, a notable exception being game, for in the Noble Boke of Cookry we find that game was to be spit roasted and served with the instruction "—and no sauce but salt and serve it". Poultry did not rate as game because it had the full sweet-sour treatment; geese were to be served with a stuffing made from the livers with parsley, hyssop, rosemary and sage, raisins, currants and the inevitable saffron and spice powder. In another recipe we are told "Sauce him with Wine and Ginger as Capons be".

Here is the fish dish whose name I quoted earlier:

Pike and Eels in Ballok* broth

To make eels and pikes in ballok broth, take and split a pike and skale him, and culpon eels small and put them in a pot. Put also green onions and cubebs and mince them and season them up with a lear of bread and put to it Cloves, Mace and powder of Cinnamon and Saffron and put there to a quantity of stock fish like unto the eels, and let the pike boil easily, and serve the whole pike for a Lord and a quarter of a pike for commons and culpans, and let them be seasoned and put the broth with the sauce upon the pike and serve it.

Stock fish was a marine fish, such as cod, which had been filleted and sun dried to keep it available for future use. It would have had a pretty strong flavour no doubt but it would keep well, and its flavour would have been masked to some extent by the other ingredients with which it was cooked.

There are a number of recipes which bear the name Lombard or Lumbarde, and which testify to the influence of Italian cookery and seasoning in England. There was Lombard mustard, Toast Lombard, Lombard stew and at a later time even Lumber Pye, which bears little resemblance to its original. Nearly all of them used as an ingredient one or other of the spice powders, and this must have been their one feature in common.

One of the main Lombard recipes was Crustade Lombarde, which was a tart described as a 'coffyn' in which was baked a mixture consisting of meat, minced dates, beef marrow and the usual season-ings of pepper, clove, mace, thickened with eggs and cream. On fast days the meat was replaced by pears, and cream was made from crushed almonds. A variant of this dish was called Leske Lombard, or Leche Lombard, the word Leske meaning sliced. This was a stiff paste of dates, with wine and cream, or in one example honey, thickened with grated bread and the usual seasonings, to which claret was added before serving. The dish was then sliced and served with a sauce containing yet more sugar, cinnamon and wine.

These crustade recipes were undoubtedly derived from Lombard cookery, and to them we owe our own mincemeat tart, which in mediaeval times was called 'Tartes of Ffleshe', or in the example I take from the Harleian MS 279, 'Tartes de Chare'.

---

*In a recipe in one of the Harleian MS this word is spelt 'Balourgly Broth'. The meaning of the word I do not know.

Season to Taste

Take fresh pork, cut it and grind it in a mortar. Add to it the yolks and whites of eggs and pass the mixture through a sieve. Then take pine nuts and currants and fry them in oil, and add them to the pork and egg mixture, with Pepper, Ginger, Cinnamon, Sugar and Saffron and salt. Make a pastry case 'coffyn' and place the mix in it, and plant the coffyn about with Pine nuts, cut dates, raisins and small birds or else hard yolks of eggs. If you use birds, first fry them in a little oil and put them in the tart, and glaze with egg or Saffron and bake.

It is sad to relate that our English mincemeat tarts contain no meat and, therefore, have no right to the name, although beef suet is retained in the recipe. It is, however, the sole survivor of the sweet-sour food of the early times, and one could not have a better example of the food which used to be served. The addition of meat could only have improved the flavour of this excellent dish.

One of the documents which illustrates the seasoning of this period is the 'Household Roll' of the Countess of Leicester, which was written as early as 1265, and is a detailed account of the household expenses incurred by the Countess. This also lists the spices one would expect to find in the store cupboard at that time, including ginger, cinnamon, pepper, clove, galingale, cummin and fennel but, surprisingly enough, no mention of mace or nutmeg, which she must have used. They varied in price from 2d. a pound for the aromatic seeds to 12s. a pound for cloves. Pepper was 1s. and sugar 1 to 2s. per pound, and these prices can be judged in the light of the price of 1s. 6d. the Countess paid for two calves, and 3s. for a calf and a sheep. Ginger was from 10d. to 2s. per pound, which is a great deal more than was paid in 1690, when the Board of Trade records give a price of 1¾d. per lb for West Indian ginger, which was then being imported.

In assessing the seasonings used in any one period, I have analysed a large number of recipes, from which one can arrive at the number of times any one of them was used. In the Noble Boke I find ginger was used in 34 percent of the recipes, pepper in 26 percent, clove in 22 percent, and cinnamon in 21½ percent of them. It must not be thought, however, that these figures may bear any relationship to the quantity which was used in a recipe. I do not think that there is any evidence that spices were used heavily, and in any case heavy use would have been unlikely in view of their relatively high price. Sugar was certainly used heavily when people could afford it, and verjuice made from crab apples or vinegar would have tempered the sweetness.

Another recipe I wish to give is the fast day one of Warden Pears in Syrup, and for general interest I will give it exactly as it appears in the Harleian MS No 4016.

Chare de Wardone

Take peer Wardons, and seth hem in wine or water; And then take hem uppe, and grinde hem in a morter, and drawe hem thorgh a streynoure with the licour; And put hem in a potte with sugur, or elles with clarefiede hony and canell (cinnamon) ynowe, and lete hem boile; And then take hit from the fire, And lete kele, and caste there-to rawe yolkes of eyren, til hit be thik, and caste thereto powder of ginger ynowe; And serue hit forth in maner of Ryse. And if hit be in lenton tyme, leve the yolkes of eyren, and lete the remnaunt boyle so longe, til it be so thikk as though hit were y-tempered with yolkes of eyren, in maner as a man sethes charge de quyns; And then serue hit forth in maner of Rys.

I hardly need add that sethe means boil, and eyren means eggs. In another recipe in the same MS there is an added instruction — "Loke that hit be poynante and also Doucet" This is probably the earliest piece of seasoning advice in the literature.

The influence of fasting and abstinence in this period is still paramount, to judge from the number of fast day recipes contained in the manuscripts. I took the trouble to look into the ecclesiastical history of fasting, and it was very interesting to see how much was written on the subject in the 16th century, and how much the opinion of one cleric differed from another. For example, Hugh Latimer, who was martyred in Queen Mary's reign in 1555, said:

"Now therefore we dwell in a realm where it has pleased the King's Majesty to make an Act (1548) that all his subjects should abstain from flesh Fridays and Saturdays and other days. If there were no such law, then we might eat as well upon Fridays as upon holidays, and this law is but a matter of policy, not of religion or holiness, and we ought to live according to the laws of the realm."

William Whitaker, born in 1547, in a disputation against the Papists says:

"The laws of Fasting were not imposed by the Apostles, but by the heretic Montanus. Secondly, I say that the rule of fasting prescribed

Season to Taste

by this Theophilus is such as the Papists themselves do not observe. He would have us, when we fast, abstain not only from flesh, but from wine. The Papists abstain from flesh indeed, but in the meantime allow other dainties, and as large a quantity of wine as you please to fast on".

Such views reflect the acute differences between protestants and catholics, and the two sides lost no opportunity of attacking each other. Nevertheless, I think both sides must have realised that the fasting practices, which varied so much from one place to another, were bringing the whole practice of fasting and abstinence into disrepute, and this must have hastened their eventual abolition. An unknown writer of the period delivered a sarcastic and perhaps not very fair attack on the Papists, which is worth quoting for the light that it throws on kinds of food that were allowed on fast days.

"Again at night, albeit Popish fasters eat no meat, yet they make such a drinking as might seem a costious kind of banqueting. Besides their white bread and fine cakes, they have their figs, raisins, almonds, apples, pears, nuts, carroways, biscuits, succet, marmalade, cherries condite, quinces and I know not what, and besides their nappy ale and heady beer, they have sundry wines, some spiced and some brewed with a cup of Ipocras at the latter end to make up their mouth withal and to finish their holy and religious fast."

Such practices as this were condemned by the catholics also, for St Hierome preached against all such belly-gods.

"What availeth it" said he "to eat no oil, and to seek about for such meats as are most dainty and hardest to come by, as dry figs, Pepper, Nuts, Dates, fine cakes, Honey and Pistacies".

Clearly the times were changing, and in the next chapter we shall see big changes in the eating habits of the people, changes that were to have far-reaching effects on the seasoning of food.

(e) The end of sweet-sour cookery

"I remember one said that there were no sallets in the lines to make the matter savoury."

HAMLET ACT II SCENE 2

If one had asked an inhabitant of London or Paris, in the year 1600, to explain the difference between sweet-sour and savoury cooking, he would not have known what you were talking about, for the word 'savoury' was not in use at this date. The Londoner would have known sweet-sour dishes, and the Parisian would have known 'Aigre-Douce', as these terms would have been applied to dishes containing more than ordinary amounts of sweet or sour ingredients.

The operative word here is 'dishes' which contain a mixture of ingredients, as opposed to roast meats and game, that came to the table direct from the fire, and with which a sauce might well have been served. There was no separate meat or sweet course to a meal, because for one thing the table furnishings, such as knives and occasionally spoons, did not provide for more than one kind of food, to say nothing of the separate pots and pans that would have been required in the kitchen.

The 17th century was one of great change and one of the most far reaching was the invention of the fork by an Italian. An English traveller, quoted in Coryat's Crudities, tells of his discovery in a journey he took in 1608.

I observed a thing in all those Italian cities and townes through the which I passed, that is not used in any other country that I saw in my travels. . . . The Italians and also most strangers there do alwayes at their meals use a little forke, when they cut their meat. For while with their knife which they hold in one hand they cut the meat out of the dish, they fasten their forke, which they hold in their other hand upon the same dish, so that whatsoever he be that sitting in the same company of any others at meale, should unadvisedly touch the dish of meat with his fingers . . . he will give cause of offence unto the company, as having transgressed the lawes of good manners. . . . The reason of this their curiosity is, because the Italian cannot by any means indure to have his dish touched with fingers, seeing that all men's fingers are not alike clean. . . .

The invention of the fork was only one of the signs that changes were taking place in the eating and serving of food. Much more important were the changes that were occurring in the kitchen, for there were now sufficient utensils available for separate meat and sweet courses to be served. The sweet or pudding course of the meal dates from the 17th century, and one of the first recipe books to contain sweet recipes is John Murrell's 'A New Booke of Cookerie' of 1617. After that date, nearly all the books contained separate chapters on sweets and puddings, and one that deserves particular mention is probably the first book by a woman, Hannah Wolley, whose 'Queen-like Closet' was first published in 1670. The title of later editions of her book gives a good idea of the ground she covered — 'The accomplish'd ladies delight in preserving, physick, beautifying and cookery'.

The changes in cookery took place gradually, and are seldom if ever mentioned specifically in the literature, only indirectly. For example, wills of the 16th and 17th centuries often mention the iron and brass cooking pots of mediaeval cookery, for these were valued possessions, which were passed on from father to son. The changes were, however, mentioned in the recipe books, by reason of the recipes often being given in alternative versions, which reflect the old method of cookery and the new. As an illustration of both the old and the new way of cookery, I take a recipe for a Chicken Pye from 'The Whole body of Cookery Dissected' by William Rabisha of 1661.

A Chicken Pye for Winter
Take half a dozen small chickens: when they are scalded, drawn and trussed for baking, season them with Nutmeg, Mace, Clove and Cinnamon and Salt, wrap up part of the seasoning in butter and put it into their bellies. Your coffin being made, lay them in, put over and between them some pieces of marrow, quartered dates, pieces of Spanish potatoes boiled, with a slice of Lemon, and half a handful of Barberries stripped, so put on butter and close up your pye; let your lear be made with white wine, sugar, a grated Nutmeg, and beaten up with the yolk of an egg, and a little drawn butter; when your pye is ready cut it up and pour it over; shake your pye well together, and cover it, you may put suckets and Chestnuts in it if you please.

This is of course a sweet-sour recipe with the sour element provided by Barberries. The alternative recipe is as follows:

Another Way
When you have trussed and seasoned your chickens with Pepper, Salt, Cloves, Mace and Nutmeg beaten, mince a good handful of Parsley, a little Thyme, and wrap it up in a little butter with some of the aforesaid seasonings and stuff the bellies of your chickens; so lay them in your Coffin prepared for them, strew over them some Lemons cut in dice, and half a handful of grapes, with some pieces of boiled artichoke, and hard cabbage leaves or lettuce, so put butter on it and close it up; when it is ready, put in a lear of white

wine and gravie, beaten up thick with a little drawn butter, and the yolk of an egg, and grated Nutmeg. Shake it together and serve it up.

Thus we pass from some six hundred years of sweet-sour cookery, to the new age of Savoury cookery, where meat or fish dishes were cooked and served separately from the sweet and sour ingredients. It took me some little time to realise the magnitude of the change that was taking place, and I made a study of the use of the word 'savoury', and from that I discovered Shakespeare's use of the word in the quotation at the head of this chapter. As Hamlet was said to have been written in 1601, this gives us one reliable date for its possible introduction. The Oxford Dictionary gives an earlier date of 1560 in its derivation from Old French — Savouré meaning sapid or fragrant, and an English meaning — 'Pleasing to the taste, appetising, agreeable'.

The Rise and influence of the Cookery Book
I must not allow the importance of the change to another kind of cookery, to mask yet another change in this period from the manuscript to the printed recipe book. Printing was very quick to replace the hand written word, although the number of books printed in the 16th century was fairly small. Apart from the early Italian cookery books, there were not many printed in England. I have seen Dawson's 'Good housewife's Jewel' of 1587, and I enjoyed reading a charming little book in the British Library, 'A Discourse on Pepper', written by Bailey in 1588. It was the 17th century which saw a big increase in the number of books published, although nothing to compare with the flood that was to appear in subsequent centuries.

I would make special mention of 'The English Housewife' by Gervase Markham in 1631, and one meets his name again and again as time goes on. Hannah Wolley's book is specially good on candying and confectionery, and she seems prepared to candy almost anything — she even tackles Nutmegs! She is one of the very few to give a recipe for making Verjuice from crab apples, and the art of making Comfits from the aromatic seeds is given in great detail.

The Rise of the Salad
This was the age when the salad became very popular. It must have been served in earlier centuries, although it is to be noted that it never appeared in recipe books until now. I cannot do better than quote what Gervase Markham says of the Sallet — as they were then called:

Season to Taste

"First then to speak of Sallets, there be some simple, some compounded, some only to furnish out the table, and some for use and adornment. Your simple Sallets are Chibols (onions) washed clean and half of the green tops cut away, and served on a fruit dish, or Chives, Escallions, Radishes, boyled Carrots, Skirrets (Sisum Sisarum, the Water-Parsnip), Parsnips and Turnips with such like served up simply. Also all young Lettuce, Cabbage Lettuce, Purslane, and divers other herbs which may be served simply without anything but a little Vinegar, Sallet Oil and Sugar.

Your compound Sallets are first the young Buds, Knots of all manner of wholesome herbs at their first springings, as Red Sage, Mint, Lettice, Violets, Marigolds, Spinage, and then served up to the table with Vinegar, Sallet oil and Sugar.

Your preserved Sallets are of two kinds, either pickled as are Cucumbers, Samphire, Purslane, Broom and suchlike; or preserved with Vinegar, as Violets, Primrose, Cowslips, Gilly flowers of all kinds, Broom flowers and, for the most part, any other flower whatsoever.

He goes on to describe more complex salads but I have given enough examples to show the kind of thing that was popular. The eminent diarist John Evelyn was an expert on the Sallet, and wrote a book about them called Acetaria — a Discourse of Sallets, which goes into great detail concerning the types of herb that he used.

Yet another kind of herb made its first appearance in this century, not in fact new in itself, but new in the generic name it was given. In a recipe for a mutton dish John Murrell instructs:

Take a Fagot of Sweete Hearbes and Grosse Pepper, strew them in a covered dish with a little salt, turn them now and then, and when they are cooked enough, put them in a clean dish with sippets of bread.

Following this mention of sweet herbs, there are two recipes, the first of which is clearly savoury as it contains no sugar, the second contains both sugar and ginger, and is not savoury.

Boyled Mutton
Mutton, 3-4 Blades of Mace, Grosse Pepper Whole Cloves, six whole Onions, Parsley, Spinage, Sorrel, Thime and grated Bread.

This is an early example of the new kind of savoury food, and alongside it is one which is quite different:

Stewed Sheeptongues
> Sheeptongues, Butter, Wine, Ginger, Cinnamon, Sugar, Salt, grated bread, handful of pickt Samphier, Lemon.

The use of Samphire is fairly rare, and Murrell must have lived, as I do, near the salt marshes where this fascinating vegetable grows in summer time near the high water mark. However, the most interesting thing about Murrell's cookery is the frequent use of the Sweete Hearbes, and his is one of the earliest books in which this term appears. In one recipe we have quite a mixture of the two kinds of cookery, for in Boyling a Knuckle of Veal, we have the following ingredients: Butter, Mace, Raisins of the Sun, Parsley, Spinache, Sorrell and a faggote of sweete hearbes. Sorrell is that salad vegetable, which has a sharp taste, that must have fitted it to be served with dishes containing sweet ingredients. Murrell's book clearly marks the watershed between sweet-sour and savoury food.

A number of other things could be said of the cookery of this century. It was William Rabisha who was clearly a master of the art of the display of food, for in his book we find instructions for serving and carving that read like poetry.

> Lift that Swan, Rear that Goose, Dismember that Heron, Unbrace that Mallard, Unlace that Coney, Sauce that Capon, Allay that Pheasant, Wing that Partridge, Display that Crane, Unjoint that Bittern, Break that Egript, Untach that Curlew, Mince that Plover, Thigh that Woodcock.

Under each bird there is a detailed description of just how the operation was to be carried out. The only one which need concern us is the Capon, of which he says: "Know well, that Capons should be sauced with one sauce, the chickens shall be sauced with green sauce or Verjuice". This, of course, was a matter of custom but the very fact that a Capon had to be 'sauced' demonstrates that the age of the sauce had arrived. Yet another recipe was a 'Charbonade' and involved the use of a Broyling Iron, not according to the recipe a 'grid iron' but a plate of iron with hooks and pricks on which you may hang the meat . . . "you set it close before the fire, so that the plate heating the meat behind, as the fire doth before, it will both the sooner and with more neatness be ready."

Now it is time to enter the modern field of savoury cookery, and to see its full flowering in the 18th and 19th centuries.

(f) The Rise of Savoury cooking

*"If you would have it savoury and not sweet, add the more spice in your
seasoning, and let your lear be only gravy."*
THE QUEEN'S ROYAL COOKERY — THOMAS HALL 1713

The quotation from Hamlet, at the head of the previous section,
seems to imply a direct connection between the introduction of the
Sallet and savoury food, although I believe that all one could claim is
that the popularity of the salad at this time underlines the change
away from the sweet food of earlier centuries. The above quotation
from Thomas Hall is perhaps the most specific reference to the big
change that was occurring, and the 1713 date puts his book among
the first of the impressive list of cookery books which started to pour
from the printing presses in this century. I have examined thirtytwo
books, and many of them have titles such as 'The Compleat Housewife', 'The Complete City and Country Cook', 'English Housewife',
'The Lady's, Housewife and Cookmaid's Assistant' and similar titles,
which show their aim to be the education of the increasing army of
housewives who were assuming their role as the leaders of the
cookery culture of the country.

Male cooks, who had been trained as apprentices in the important
kitchens of noble homes up and down the country, were still with us
of course, but in those days, long before the opening of the first school
of cookery, it was the housewives who needed to be trained, and the
only means of training them was by means of the cookery book. I
have selected five books, all by women, almost all of which reached or
exceeded ten separate editions, which gives some idea of their popularity.

Author	Title	Number of editions
Eliza Smith	The Complete Housewife	1728. 18 editions
Hannah Glasse	The Art of Cookery	1747. 14 editions
Elizabeth Moxon	English Housewifry	1749. 14 editions
Elizabeth Raffald	The Experienced House-Keeper	1769. 16 editions
Charlotte Mason	The Lady's Assistant	1775. 9 editions

The cookery situation in this century must be seen against the
background of the rapid rise in population at this time, with such
towns as Bath, Harrogate or Edinburgh, to say nothing of the larger
cities, each with their rows or handsome crescents of substantial
houses, each with their kitchens and pantries to house their cooks
and serving maids, who were needed to staff them.

There is little doubt that much of the cookery advice was beyond the understanding of many of the cooks of the day, which may explain why they were mostly addressed to the housewife rather than the cook herself, who would often have lacked the ability to read, and we shall see the full effects of the great shortage of trained cooks when we look at cookery in the Victorian age.

In the early books of the century we still find recipes given in two versions, for example, Eliza Smith gives a recipe for Savoury Lamb Pye alongside one for a sweet Lamb Pye, the latter containing raisins and currants, sugar and citron, orange and lemon peel. Thomas Hall himself gave many of his recipes in two versions and, more important, he emphasises the importance of the gravy in savoury food. His quotation continues "—let your Lear be only gravy, or the baking bones and some meat, in Claret wine as before. This you may observe in all other meats betwixt the Lears of sweet and savoury".

Lear is the English equivalent of the French word 'liaison', which is most used today to mean a thickening for a soup or a sauce. Hall must have been as much at home with one kind of cookery as with the other, for he gives one recipe for a Lumber Pye, a debased Lombard recipe, which contains neither Cinnamon nor Saffron but nevertheless does contain veal, beef suet, eggs and cream, cloves, mace, Sweet Herbs and sugar baked in a dish. At the other extreme he gives an example of an early savoury dish, "a good strong savoury broth as it was made for our Queen on mornings". It contained veal, beef, mutton or chicken, onion, garlic, parsley, thyme, mint, balm, coriander seeds, pepper, clove and very little saffron.

It is a woman, Hannah Glasse, however, who for me dominates the new scene of savoury food, because of her clear understanding of the art of seasoning food, and she is the first person, male or female, who enunciates what I believe to be the essence of the art of seasoning food in two statements, which she made in her chapter on 'made dishes'. This is what she said:

"—and as to brown sauce, take great care no fat swims to the top, and that it be all smooth alike, and about as thick as good cream, *and not to taste of one thing more than another. As to Pepper and Salt, season to your palate, and do not put too much of either, for that will take away the fine flavour of everything.*"

The other statement which she made in a section on making soups and broths was as follows:

Season to Taste

"You must observe in all broths and soups that one thing does not taste more than another; but that the taste be equal, and it has a fine agreeable relish, according to what you design it for."

I have emphasised both her statements, because, simple though they are, nobody else until this time, and very few people afterwards, have ever thought it necessary to state what I consider to be the very heart of seasoning practice. I shall be saying much more about what I call the matter of Flavour Balance when I reach the final 'How to do it' section of this book.

The neutral or, in other words, entirely non acid food, which is essential for the development of the savoury taste, entirely dominates the type of ingredients which may be used and, apart from the herbs and spices, to which we shall come in a moment, there are four foods which are harmonious with savoury food, that we find are increasingly used. These are first onions, second mushrooms, and third and fourth oysters and anchovies. It is perhaps surprising that these latter fish foods can go with meat but this is indeed the case, and some of the most delicious foods I know come into this category.

The mushroom is important, and as I have done not a little research work on the flavour of the mushroom, perhaps I might say a little. The mushroom has what I can only call a delicate and 'small' flavour, and everything possible has to be done to retain its flavour during cooking, and to use it with harmonious ingredients. Unfortunately, mushrooms vary widely in their flavour with their variety, and as bad luck will have it, the variety most used in commerce has a weak flavour, it being bred more for its resistance to disease than for its strength of flavour. There is a pressing need for the growing of fungi of better flavour than the cultivated varieties we have at present, although I have to admit that at least what we have is available all the year round, whereas our ancestors had to gather mushrooms in the autumn, and preserve them for use during the year. A favourite means of doing this was to make them into Mushroom Ketchup, and another writer of the time was Elizabeth Raper who, in a domestic recipe gave the following method of pickling mushrooms.

To Pickle Mushrooms

Take the buttons and rub them with a clean dry cloth, the open ones to be peeled and the gills taken out, put them in a saucepan with a little salt, and over a slow fire when they boil let them boil pretty fast for 5 or 6 minutes, until they feel tough. Then strain them out (save the liquor) and lay them in a clean cloth covered over till dry. Put them in your glasses. Take the best vinegar, a little Mace, a few Cloves, some white Pepper, Nutmeg, and a race of Ginger, and put to the vinegar with the liquor the mushrooms were boiled in, and boil them together for a few minutes. When cold put this pickle into the glasses over the mushrooms to cover them.

Elizabeth Raper would, of course, have used the field mushrooms, and would have used the preserve to add flavour to her savoury dishes.

From the point of view of seasoning, what we now have to examine is which of the herbs, seeds and spices are harmonious with savoury food. I mentioned that in the previous century we saw the first mention of a new term 'sweet herbs' but only one writer seems to have identified which herbs were regarded as in the category of 'sweet'. This was Robert May who, in a recipe for marinating Neat's tongues (Oxtongues), said:

"Next have a bundle of Sweet Herbs, as Tyme, Rosemary, Bay Leaves, Sage Leaves, Winter Savory, Sweet Marjoram, and Parsley — and bind them into a bundle every sort by itself, and all into one.

It is not until nearly a century later that we find the next identification of sweet herbs, and it was Hannah Glasse, who in a recipe for roasting a hare said:

"Make a pudding thus; take a quarter of a pound of beef Suet, as much crumb of bread, a handful of Parsley chopped fine, some sweet herbs of all sorts such as Basil, Marjoram, Winter Savory and a little Thyme—"

Her list differs from that of Robert May, and she omits mention of the rather strong tasting herbs, such as bay, rosemary and sage. I do not think that I need add anything to what I said in the chapter on herbs, other than to say that in my view there is a difference between such herbs as basil, savory and marjoram, which have a certain similarity of flavour, that may be described as 'sweet'. While they are highly aromatic, they are nevertheless not strong tasting herbs like sage or even rosemary, which have a way of imposing their flavour over and above that of herbs with a milder flavour. This is quite important when we consider the balance of flavour in a dish.

The aromatic seeds are not used very much if at all in savoury dishes, and their use is confined to sweet dishes and to the making of

Comfits, which were handed round after a meal, the seeds used being aniseed, caraway and dill, and sometimes coriander. It is interesting, however, that the great user of aromatic seeds, curry, does not figure much in the recipe books. Hannah Glasse gives a recipe for 'Currey-the Indian way' but the seeds are conspicuous by their absence! The only seasonings she used were ginger, turmeric and pepper.

The usage of spices in the savoury food of the period is considerable, and I quote Hannah Glasse again only because I have made a detailed study of her recipes. In her chapter on 'made' dishes, she uses pepper in 51 percent of the recipes, nutmeg in 28 percent, and clove in 25 percent. Of the 219 recipes in the chapter, ginger and cinnamon were not used at all, as is to be expected in savoury recipes. I take one of her recipes at random — 'To ragoo a breast of Veal', to illustrate her seasoning:

> Take your breast of Veal, put it into a large stewpan, put in a bundle of sweet herbs, an onion, some black and white Pepper, a blade or two of Mace, two or three Cloves, a very little piece of Lemon peel, and just cover it with water; etc, etc.

You will see that in this recipe, and many others like it, she is using the spices in a combination, much the same combination as in the sweet-sour days with the major exception of the sweet spices.

What I am going to advocate in this book is that we should return to this type of seasoning in order to achieve a major improvement in the flavour of our savoury food. Hannah Glasse's seasoning and that of the other writers of this century, which was the same, died out in the following century for reasons that will appear in the next section. It will be my intention and purpose to demonstrate just how I use this type of seasoning in my own cookery, and how we can avoid the pitfalls that caused 18th century cookery to fall into decay as it did in the 19th century. Before we can do that, there are a few other aspects of the cookery of the period we must examine, together with one or two examples of the recipes that were in use.

Thomas Hall was probably the first cookery writer to prescribe exact quantities of ingredients, and he was clearly a cook of some experience. It was he who tells of a way of conveying the flavour of caraway in a recipe for "Lady H—'s method of making a Caraway cake", which involves using ¾lb of Caraway Comfits. These Comfits were very popular and of course were mostly sugar but, nevertheless, with the pervading odour of the aromatic seed which they contained.

It is in this century that we start to see an increasing use of the relatively new spice capsicum. I say relatively new because it only appeared after its discovery in America. At last Europeans had an alternative way of obtaining hotness in a food, and some people are very fond of the pungency which they provide. Such a one must have been the same Elizabeth Raper, whose recipe for mushroom pickle I gave earlier. She also provides the following unique recipe for a condiment she calls Caveachi:

> Take half an ounce of Caveachi (the yellow powder is the best) and a quarter ounce of Coriander seeds and 8 to 10 cloves of Garlic, put these in a quart of good Vinegar and set it to boil slowly, or rather only to simmer till 'tis near half wasted, then strain it through a fine sieve or piece of muslin, put it in a bottle and keep for use, its very good to mix in a fish sauce or anything savoury.

I suppose I should not be surprised that there was no mention of the proper name of Caveachi, which of course is capsicum, or more usually Cayenne pepper, although perhaps this name dates from a later date.

I should I think explain that the only reason why I have used Elizabeth Raper's work is my interest in the two recipes I have quoted. Her book is not one of the standard ones and anyone who wishes to study the recipes of this period should consult one of the books I have mentioned. It's time that I should choose an illustration of the new savoury cooking, and I have chosen first to give Elizabeth Raffald's Beef à la Mode.

> Take the bone out of a rump of Beef, lard the top with Bacon, then make a forcemeat of four ounces of Marrow, two heads of Garlic, the crumbs of a penny loaf, a few Sweet Herbs chopped small, Nutmeg, Pepper and Salt to your taste, and the yolks of four eggs well beat, mix it up, and stuff your beef where the bone came out, and several places in the lean part, skewer it round and bind it about with a fillet, put it in a pot with a pint of red wine, and tie it down with paper, bake it in the oven for three hours; when it comes out, if you want to eat it hot, skim the fat off the gravy, and add half an ounce of Morels, a spoonful of pickled Mushrooms, thicken it with flour and butter, dish up your Beef and pour on your Gravy, lay it round with Forcemeat Balls, and send it up.

Such a recipe covers several of the points I have already made but I must say one word about the use of beef marrow. It has been used very extensively in cookery over the ages and it seems a pity that it is seldom used today. I have done quite a lot of research on the flavouring properties of Marrow, and it is of the greatest value in adding the inimitable 'sweet' flavour of meat. I use inverted commas to make sure nobody can think I refer to the sweetness of sugar; it is most difficult to describe flavour and I know no other quality than this 'sweetness' to use for just one of the flavour components of meat and particularly of beef. I believe that I know of what this flavour consists but that is another story too scientific to be told here.

Having talked about the flavour of meat, I think I cannot do better than give Hannah Glasse's own recipe for a gravy for general use, as it contains all the elements necessary to achieve a flavour of a very high order.

Gravy for Turkey, Fowl or Ragoo
Take a pound of lean beef, cut and hack it well, then flour it well, put a piece of butter as big as a hen's egg in a stew pan; when it is melted put in your beef, fry it on all sides a little brown, then pour in three pints of boiling water, and a bundle of sweet herbs, two or three blades of Mace, three or four Cloves, twelve whole Peppercorns, a little piece of Carrot, a little piece of crust of bread toasted brown; cover it close, and let it boil till there is about a pint or less; then season it with salt and strain it off.

This is only one means of making gravy or stock, and the only comment I wish to make on it, is to draw attention to the piece of bread crust toasted brown. This is an addition to meat flavour which I have found used throughout history, and the cooks of history just cannot be wrong.

We now have to deal with a period of history which in some ways is very odd, because in the 19th century, strange to relate, cookery reached its greatest heights but also, alas, its greatest depths of degradation. We shall talk of the depths first, under an appropriate name.

(g) The Age of Hash

" She was so little equal to Rebecca's Puddings and Rebecca's Hashes – that she was constrained to send her brothers in the evening for biscuits and buns."

FANNY PRICE. JANE AUSTEN'S MANSFIELD PARK

We leave the 18th century as the writers were busy churning out their cookery books, with the object of trying to train the domestic cooks and housekeepers of Georgian England. The cookery of the 19th century can only be understood if it is appreciated that it developed in two quite different directions. The cookery books show this clearly, because they are of two different types; the first were written to appeal to the large households of Regency England, and were often written by French chefs who worked and made their homes in England, or who had served in royal households. Such a one was Eustace Ude, whose 'French Chef' was published in 1813, or Charles Francatelli, chef to Queen Victoria, whose 'Modern Cook' appeared in 1845. Ude in the preface to his work says: "I venture to affirm that cookery in England, when well done, is superior to that of any in the world". I think he was probably right insofar as it applies to the London clubs, some of the more important taverns, such as the London Tavern, and many of the large noble homes up and down the countryside.

The second category is represented by books that were designed to appeal to the huge number of ordinary domestic cooks who were trying to serve the average household of the well-to-do merchant, cleric or other official of the rapidly growing towns and cities of urban England. One of these was Isabella Beeton's mammoth 'Household Management', published in 1861, and yet it also contained the sort of recipes which were contained in Ude's book, for it was the first of the cookery compendia. One could find in it Ude's Turtle soup recipe or Beef à la Flamande next door to an entirely different kind of recipe. Her preface makes her intention clear:

'For the matter of the recipes, I am indebted in some measure, to many correspondents of "The Englishwoman's Domestic Magazine", who have obligingly placed at my disposal their formulae for many original preparations. A large private circle has also rendered me considerable service. A diligent study of the works of the best modern writers on cookery was also necessary to the faithful fulfillment of my task. Friends in England, Scotland, Ireland, France and Germany have also materially aided me. I have paid great attention to those recipes which come under the heading of Cold Meat Cookery.'

To judge from the above quotation, Jane Austen must have been well aware of the hashes which were being served in towns and cities all over the country, and we are reminded of the great gulf which existed between the kitchens of Fanny Price's Mansfield Park and those of the backstreets of Portsmouth. However, the reason for the hashes did not start to become clear to me until I took the trouble to look up 'The Englishwoman's Domestic Magazine', published in the 1830's and mentioned by Isabella Beeton in her preface. Each of the issues contained an article by an unnamed cookery correspondent, one of which contained the following revealing passage.

"Our object in the present work is to give a cheap, wholesome and palatable method of cookery that shall come within the reach of every class in the community. A great variety of relishing, nutritive, and even elegant dishes, may be prepared from the most homely materials, which may not only be rendered more nourishing, but be made to go much further in a large family than they usually do. . . . With regard to 'made dishes', as the horrible imitations of French cookery prevalent among the middle classes in England are termed, we must admit that they are very unwholesome. All the juices are boiled out of the meat, which is swimming in a greasy heterogeneous compound, disgusting to the sight, and seasoned strongly with spice and Cayenne Pepper, that it would inflame the stomach of an ostrich."

In another article the same unknown writer attacked "the staid elderly females" who, he said, posed as cooks in middle class Victorian households. "These elderly dram-drinking persons, thirsty souls on account of the heat they say, though they most frequently increase the kitchen fire to a needless ten-fold degree of intensity—". Now this is all very unfair to the cooks of those days, and makes no mention of the true reason for the malaise in middle class cookery, *which was that there were no schools of cookery in the first half of the century to supply the pressing need for cooks for the rapidly expanding Victorian households.*

Another article admits that the cookery of Ude was beyond the capability of the readers of the magazine . . . "Yet Monsieur Ude's work is too scientific for our readers; it presupposes too much knowledge in the tyro who has occasion to examine its pages but, if schools were to be established for rearing teachers of the culinary art, Monsieur Ude's book would become the textbook, and the eloquent author would no doubt be raised to the chair of Regius Professor." It is also clear from another article that some of the doctors of the metropolis were against the 'made dishes' of the cookery books, and urged their patients to forsake these greasy 'made' dishes, which were no doubt prepared by inexperienced cooks, in favour of a good plain joint.

This brings one to the other part of the hash conundrum, for it must be realised that a revolution in cookery was taking place in early Victorian Britain. A huge expansion in the population was taking place, with the towns and cities growing at a rapid pace and, to feed the massive town populations, the new railways were reaching out from the towns to convey food of all kinds from the surrounding countryside. The most important food was meat, large joints of it at most reasonable prices, which were roasted in Victorian ovens on Sunday, eaten cold on Monday, and on succeeding days of the week made into hash, toad-in-the-hole, and many other 'cold meat dishes'.

Now there is nothing inherently difficult about cooking a roast joint, although it was no doubt sometimes grossly overcooked, and the particular service rendered by Mrs Beeton was to collate the new recipes for 'cold meat cookery' and present them to a huge public, who were avid to know how to use up the cold leftovers from Sunday's joint. A feature of these recipes is that many of them specified the addition of stock or water to provide the proper consistency to minced cold meat but, alas, the stock from the Sunday joint would not often have been kept to add to the dish a few days later, and it is the addition of stock that makes such dishes palatable.

Before I bury cold meat cookery in the oblivion that it deserves, I feel that I must say a few words about Isabella Beeton in the light of the knowledge we now have of the history of cookery and of seasoning. It is no service to cooks to say that cookery is an easy art, and it should be recognised that it is a complex and quite difficult art, which involves the use of the highest critical faculties. Isabella was the young wife of a young publisher Samuel Beeton, who had already published a great many books before his wife was called on to prepare her one thousand page work. She says in her preface "I must frankly own, that if I had known before hand that this book would have cost me the labour which it has, I should never have been courageous enough to start it". In a strange way it was a huge book because cookery was such a big subject. There was no need for it to have contained such recipes as Turtle Soup or Beef à la Flamande, for there were plenty of other books which gave the same advice but what it did provide were the recipes for cold meat cookery which were not provided by other books, so that its success was well deserved. It is sad to record that she died from puerpural fever, four years after the publication of her book, just at the time when her husband became bankrupt and the valuable copyright fell into other hands. Her posthumous fame shows that the middle class housewife responded to her advice, and it is not for us to regret her concentration on cold meat cookery, which carries the art of seasoning very little further. I had to tell her story because it is part of the whole picture of cookery and of seasoning on which we are engaged.

It is only fair to give a recipe for Hash, which I have taken from another writer of that time, Mrs Rundell, whose 'New System of Domestic Cookery' ran into many editions. I take it from the 1876 edition when the art of hashing must have been in its heyday.

Beef Hash

Cut Beef that has been dressed into slices, put them in a stewpan, with slices of pickle, either Walnuts or Onions; then make a sauce with chopped shallots or onions, passed with a bit of butter over a slow fire, till nearly done; after which add a pint of Veal stock or Gravy, and a little Ketchup. Boil it ten minutes, season with Cayenne Pepper and Salt; then strain it to the Beef, let it stew gently till thoroughly hot, and add a small quantity of browning.

Now this would have been a tolerable recipe if the pint of Veal stock or gravy had been used but one has to ask whatever was the use of buying more meat to make the stock or gravy to use up meat that had already lost its own meat juices? In practice, the meat stock or gravy would rarely have been used in the recipe, and water perhaps with the addition of a little meat extract would have been used in its place.

Now it is our pleasurable task to look at the other side of British cookery, and to see what Monsieur Ude and other eminent cooks were doing when Rebecca was making her Hash.

(h) The Age of Elegance

"No particular herb or spice should be allowed to predominate powerfully in these compositions; but the whole of the seasonings should be taken in such quantity only as will produce an agreeable savour when they are blended together"
ELIZA ACTON — MODERN COOKING FOR PRIVATE FAMILIES 1845

Cookery books published in this century catered for three quite separate needs. The first, which we have already examined, was a simple type of cookery for the artisan or the tradesman, and consisted of the cold meat cookery of Mrs Beeton, which was based on the joints of meat which were so plentifully available. The second type of book was for high class domestic cookery, and several written in the previous century were still being reprinted. New ones were also appearing, of which undoubtedly the most outstanding was Eliza Acton's Modern Cookery for Private Families, which was published in 1845.

There was, however, a third type of cookery book being published at this time, devoted to the needs of the catering or professional cook who served in noble homes, or in the Clubs, or in the new kind of tavern, such as the London Tavern, which were the precursors of the modern restaurant. There were quite a number of such books, of which I select two for mention, first 'The French Cook' by Eustace Ude, which ran to at least fourteen editions from 1813 to 1841. The other book was by Charles Francatelli, one time cook to Queen Victoria, whose book, first published in 1861, ran to at least twenty-eight editions, under various titles.

I called this chapter the Age of Elegance because side by side with the hash, that was being served up in the majority of homes, another style of cookery was being developed, which was of a high order. Monsieur Eustace Ude was one of those commanding figures who was fond of delivering moral advice and high sounding statements, and it is worth quoting what he said of the standard of English cookery:

"As cookery originated in France,* it is not astonishing to find most of the names of French extraction — Soupe à la Reine, à la Condé, à la Bonne Femme, etc, Entrées à la Richelieu, à la Villeroi, à la Dauphine, etc. Why should we not see in this book the names of those true epicures who have honoured good cookery by their approbation, and have by their good taste and liberality elevated it to a great superiority in this country over what it is now in France? I will venture to affirm, that cookery in England, when well done, is superior to that of any in the world".

Or again, his reference to Dr Johnson:

"The greatest of modern moralists, Dr Johnson not only derived much enjoyment from the dinner table, but had the manliness to avow it. This is as it should be. Though a Frenchman, I revere the memory of the illustrious English philosopher who paid so much honour to the art which I profess, and who promised to write a

*Rather a sweeping statement this — it's a matter for argument that it originated in Lombardy!

book about it."

Ude, however, is equally right in his cookery judgements, as for example in the advice he gives regarding the importance of the broth or stock in the flavour of food:

"It is on a good first Broth, and good sauce that you must depend for good cookery. If you have left this work to persons who are negligent, you can make but indifferent work."

My own experience coincides with that of Ude, and I have found in my own research work that it is indeed the broth or meat stock on which the quality of dishes mainly depends. Food can possess what I have come to regard as Positive Flavour quality, and by this I mean a flavour that is present and can be recognised by trained palates in its own right. If this elusive flavour quality was damaged during the cooking of the food, or damaged by lack of freshness, then its absence will result in food of only Negative Flavour. All foods possess Positive Flavour initially, for example, freshly baked bread has it to a marked degree; fruit can have it if there is a proper balance between its sweetness and its sourness, and its ripeness has produced its typical aroma. Fish can certainly have it, in the typical sweetness of really freshly caught fish but it is highly perishable, and can be lost almost overnight, and can certainly be lost by long storage in a refrigerator. However, above all other foods, meat has this flavour quality in the highest degree.

I think it would be useful for me to say something about the flavour of meat at this point, before we look at examples of Ude's and Acton's work. The flavour of meat has a number of components. One of these is displayed when meat is roasted in front of a hot fire. Another component is evident when a game bird or the cooked carcass of a game bird is simmered down to provide the characteristic flavour of game for a soup but perhaps the main component is the meatiness, that resides in the aqueous contents of the meat cells, and which is released by cooking as stock or broth, and whose release is hastened by piercing the meat with a sharp knife. This is the stock, which Ude rightly says, is the foundation of good cookery. *

Ude's book contains many other pieces of good advice, for example his advice about the inadvisability of clearing a stock, because of the loss of aroma that this entails. In his day, a really clear stock was vitally necessary for such soups as Julienne, Petite Marmite or clear

*The author's own recipe for meat stock will be found in the next section of this book.

Oxtail soup, and for the supreme Turtle Soup, of which more later. He objected to the practice of clearing a stock with white of egg, which he maintained was due to the carelessness of the one who prepared it, because he knew that aroma was lost by doing this. He was right in stressing that fat and oil should be kept as low as possible in a recipe, for too much fat produces a sickly taste, and only sufficient should be used to act as a carrier of the essential oils of herbs and spices, as well as to provide the smooth texture of a cream sauce.

Compared with Ude, Eliza Acton, the domestic cook, was different mainly, I think, because she was talking to a different audience. She realised that recipes should be accurately measured for correct results to be obtained every time. This is what she said on the subject:

> "Many indifferent cooks pique themselves on never doing any-thing by rule, and the consequence of their throwing together at random (or by guess as they call it) the ingredients which ought to be proportioned with exceeding exactness, is repeated failure in all they attempt to do. Long experience, with a very correct eye, it is true, enable a person to dispense with weights and measures without hazarding the success of their operation but it is an exper-iment which the learner will do better to avoid."

She, however, did much more for cookery than her insistence on exactness of method, for she, with Hannah Glasse of almost a century earlier, understood the all important principle of flavour balance, which is fundamental to good seasoning, and she was prepared to commit herself to writing about it. I used her advice in the quotation at the head of this chapter.

Let me now give a few examples of the cookery of the time, paying particular attention to seasoning. I think I shall give Ude's recipe for his Velouté or Bechamel Sauce. I shall use his own words, only explaining that a 'Tammy' is a fine hair sieve, and that 'glaze' is a meat stock evaporated to the consistency of treacle.

Velouté or Bechamel, a New Method

As it is not customary in England to allow a principal cook, six assistants or deputies, for half a dozen or even ten entrées, I have thought it incumbent upon me to abridge to the best of my ability, the various preparations of sauces, etc. Put into a stewpan a knuckle of veal, some slices of ham, four or five pounds of beef, the legs and loins of a fowl, all the trimmings of meat or of game that you have, and moisten them with boiled water sufficient to cover

Season to Taste

half the meat. Make it sweat gently on a slow fire, till the meat is done through; this you may ascertain by thrusting your knife into it; if no blood follows, it is time to moisten with boiling water, sufficient to cover all the meat. Then season with a bundle of Parsley and green onions, a Clove, half a Bayleaf, Thyme, a little salt, and trimmings of Mushrooms. When the sauce has boiled long enough to let the knuckle be well done, skim off all the fat, strain it through a silken sieve, and boil down this consommé till it is nearly glaze; next take four spoonfuls of very fine flour, dilute it with three pints of very good cream, in a stew pan big enough to hold the cream, consommé, flour, etc. Boil the flour and cream on a slow fire. When it boils pour in the consommé, and continue to boil it on a slow fire if the sauce be thick but, on the contrary, if the sauce be thin, on a quick fire, in order to thicken it. Season with salt but put no Pepper. No white Sauce admits Pepper, except when you introduce into it something fine. (This is because of the grains of ground pepper which might be visible.) This sauce should be very thick. Put it into a white basin through a Tammy, and keep it in the larder out of the dust.

This sauce is the foundation, if I may so speak, of all sorts of little sauces, especially in England, where white sauces are preferred. On this account I seldom adopt the former method. In summer I was unable to procure any butter fit for use, and accordingly I was forced to do without, and found that my sauce was the better for it. This sauce should always be kept very thick, as you can thin it whenever you please, either with stock-broth or cream. If too thin, it could not be used for so many purposes.

I have given this extract in some detail, not because it is suitable for modern cookery but to emphasise the great importance placed on the use of a properly constructed meat stock by a master of the art of cookery. His comment on the omission of butter from his recipe has to be seen in the light of the large amount of cream which he uses, and it does not surprise me that the omission of butter improved his recipe.

Acton's spicing is about the average for this period, consisting of pepper, clove and mace, and the herbs, which she calls 'savoury herbs', consist of parsley, thyme, winter savory, basil and sweet marjoram. Exactly the same goes for the sweet herbs of Hannah Glasse. She uses lemon thyme in some of her recipes, which is the herb I mostly use. Her book is to be highly recommended for modern use, although I do not think that her method of measuring the seasonings by using fractions of a saltspoonful is to be recommended. In the third section of this book I shall be proposing another method of overcoming this difficulty. She has a chapter on what she calls 'store sauces', which include an apple chutney, and Tomata Catsup (this is the curious spelling used at that time for tomato). The fact that she lists these sauces need cause no surprise, for I have already pointed out that a sharp vinegar-based sauce is a perfectly legitimate addition to savoury food.

One example of Acton's work is her small Marrow Crustades dressed in Marrow:

> Cut very evenly from a thin stale loaf slices nearly an inch and a half thick, and with a plain cutter, scarcely more than half the size, mark out the space which is afterwards to be hollowed out from it. Melt some clarified marrow in a saucepan and when it begins to boil put in the patties, and fry them gently until they are equally coloured of a pale golden brown. Drain the marrow, take out the rounds which have been marked on the top, scooping out part of the inside crumb, but leave them thick enough to contain the gravy of the preparation to be put into them. Fill them with any good patty meat and serve them very hot on a napkin.

Marrow confers an excellent flavour on meat dishes, and for this reason it has been appreciated for many centuries as a flavour enhancer. Marrow bones were also used as a dish — you will recall the 'Mary-bones' of Chaucer's tales.

I promised to give the recipe for Ude's Turtle Soup, which is dependent for its flavour on the herb basil. It was not invented by Ude because its recipe is also given by John Mollard of the London Tavern in his 'Art of Cookery' of 1801. I have omitted the rather tedious description of the preparation of the turtles, whose meat contributes little specific flavour to the stock. As a turtle is unlikely to be available, I suggest the stock is made with leg of beef, and small pieces of turtle meat can be added to the soup by purchasing a tin of turtle meat, obtainable as Calipash or Calipee. Here is the relevant part:

Turtle Soup
> Lay a few slices of ham on the bottom of a very large stewpan. Lay over the ham two or three knuckles of veal, according to the size of the Turtle, and over the veal the inside flesh of a turtle, and the members over the whole. Then partly moisten it with water in

which you are boiling the shell, and sweat it thoroughly. You can ascertain if the meat be thoroughly done, by thrusting your knife into the fleshy part of the meat. If no blood issue, moisten it again in the liquor in which the bones, etc, have been boiling: put in a large bunch of all such sweet herbs as are used in the cooking of a turtle: Sweet Basil, Sweet Marjoram, Lemon Thyme, Winter Savory, two or three Bay leaves, Common Thyme, a handful of Parsley and green onions, and a large onion stuck with six Cloves. Let the whole be thoroughly done.

When the stock is completed to his satisfaction, he skims it with great care, for the soup is to be clear and there must be no scum or fat, which might cause cloudiness. He then adds a whole bottle of a good Madeira wine but remember he was cooking a whole turtle, so the batch size was fairly big. The last instruction was — "before you send it up, squeeze the juice of two or three lemons with a little Cayenne Pepper and pour it into the soup.

The most interesting part from our viewpoint is the seasoning. Many chefs used the full gamut of spices, such as clove, pimento, Long Pepper,* black pepper and mace, but Ude uses only clove and, although he does not say so, I think the reason for this was that he did not wish to risk over-seasoning and thus masking the flavour of the basil and the other herbs which are almost entirely responsible for the characteristic flavour of the soup together, of course, with the Madeira wine. There is a real danger in overseasoning a dish by using too many herbs or spices. When I am using wine in a dish, I rarely use any more than one other group of the vegetable seasonings, that is to say, wine and herbs, or wine and spices but not wine, herbs and spices. I believe that many a dish has been spoilt by trying to improve on perfection, to gild the lily, and this is very dangerous in the art of seasoning.

I have two other recipes I wish to give, which come from the pen of another chef W. H. Brand, who founded the business in which I served, and who was another of those who served his apprenticeship in the royal kitchens, and afterwards wrote a book — 'The Complete Modern Cook' (in 1834). One is his game stock, in which the flavour

---

*Long Pepper was one of the several varieties of pepper which were in occasional use. *Piper longum* was in the form of a catkin and, in addition to its pungency, it possessed a slight aroma of ginger.

Season to Taste

of the game resides in the meat rather than, as in the case of other meats, in the stock. The carcass in game is of great importance to flavour.

Consommé of Game, or Game stock

Put the backs of roasted Pheasants or Partridges or Grouse on some pieces of veal in a stew pan, the carcases of rabbits may be added. Put also a few slices of ham and a seasoned faggot, that is, Bay leaves, Basil, and a couple of Cloves and a blade of Mace tied into a bunch. If you are about to use truffles with game, add the parings, with mushrooms to your stock. Add water or better still Beef stock, enough just to cover the game carcasses. Simmer for an hour or so and strain through a sieve.

I would not use any mace in such a stock but that is a matter of opinion. I like to retain in the Consommé the little bits and pieces of game within the soup, because I think they reinforce the flavour.

The other recipe of Brand's is a most useful one, because it uses up the odd mushrooms and mushroom parings, which are often available in a kitchen. It is also a most useful example of flavour harmony, about which I shall soon be talking. I fear that there is grave danger, however, of confusing this preparation with the commonly used Fines Herbes used as a seasoning in egg and other dishes.

Fines Herbes

Four tablespoonfuls of chopped mushroom, with lemon juice squeezed over them, or they will turn black; a tablespoonful of chopped Parsley; Four eschallots, chopped very fine, or a piece of onion. Put in a stewpan on the fire a piece of butter as large as an egg, with the onion or eschallots, stir a few minutes, put in the parsley; stir again a couple of minutes, with the addition of a bay leaf, a little Pepper and salt, add your mushrooms and stir the whole over the fire about ten minutes more. Take out your Bayleaf and put your Fines Herbes in a Jelly pot for use.

The flavour harmony of this recipe arises from the use of the four ingredients — butter, mushrooms, onions and parsley, all of which blend beautifully with each other. The effect of cooking them together is to drive off the natural moisture of the mushrooms, which improves the keeping quality of the mixture, hence Brand's instruction to put it in a pot for future use. I use it as a garnish to serve with a grilled steak.

So ends my short review of the Age of Elegance. There are many other books of cookery by people of worth but those I have mentioned are probably as good as any and probably well representative of the quite different types of cookery they practised. The cookery of the period cannot be understood unless it is realised that there is a great difference in standard between the cookery of the great houses and the clubs, and that of the great mass of the people who were enjoying the benefits of the limitless quantities of cheap meat brought to the cities by the new railways.

Ude's kind of cookery was undoubtedly of a high order but it had within it the seeds of its own decay, for it was too specialised to be practised outside the inner circle of the noble homes, clubs and restaurants in which it was served. Beeton merely recorded the cookery which was going on around her, and as she was not herself an experienced cook it is doubtful whether she herself had much idea of what such haute cuisine entailed. She, however, was of the class which practised popular cookery, and that is why she made particular reference to cold meat cookery in her preface. She lived too close to the times of which she wrote to be able to distinguish between the two quite different kinds of cookery that had developed in Victorian England.

Perhaps there were a certain number of houses who served both beef hash and turtle soup on occasions. Certainly Eliza Acton, who was an experienced cook, gave the recipes for both of them. What is quite certain, however, is that the seasoning practice of the 18th century, of which Hannah Glasse wrote, did not survive the Victorian hash revolution. It was never understood by the cooks who had never had the advantage of being apprenticed to a large and busy kitchen, and it is no real surprise that all they could produce was 'a greasy heterogeneous compound, disgusting to the sight, and seasoned so strongly with Spice and Cayenne Pepper that it would have inflamed the stomach of an ostrich'!

What stage has cookery reached now? Each town and city is well supplied with excellent schools of cookery, which have raised the standard of cookery sometimes to heights undreamt of in Isabella Beeton's day. Cookery, however, is a big subject, and few cooks know how to use the little bottles of herbs and spices which decorate our kitchens. In the third section of this book, I intend to use the knowledge we have gathered from the past, and propose a method of seasoning, which I have developed, that not only takes account of the expertise of our ancestors but also allows for the convenience of the average domestic cook. The kitchen is a very different place today from what it was when seasoning was last practised in the 18th century, and we have many aids which just were not available to Hannah Glasse and Elizabeth Raffald. Let me leave this account of Regency cookery by quoting what Eustace Ude said about cookery and the art of seasoning:

> "Cookery cannot be done like Pharmacy. The Pharmacist is obliged to weigh every ingredient that he employs, as he does not like to taste it; the cook on the other hand must taste often, as the reduction increases the flavour. It would be blind work indeed without tasting: the very best soups and entrees, in which you have omitted to put salt, are entirely without flavour; seasoning in cookery is what chords are to music; the best instrument, in the hands of the best professor, without it being in tune, is insipid."

Part III — *The Seasoning of Food Today*

(a) The nature of the problem

The Fourth Article is that as sovereign mistress of your house, you know how to order dinners, suppers, dishes and courses, and have knowledge of spices.

THE GOODMAN OF PARIS 1363

My grand-daughter, when taking an A level cookery course, asked me whether I could tell her anything about the flavour of food. She went on to say that while her teachers were expert in nearly all aspects of cookery, they seemed to know next to nothing about flavour. I believe that her criticism is justified but I do not blame her teachers, because nothing has been written on the subject. Flavour is what seasoning is all about, for we cannot, or at least we should not, add seasonings before we have assessed the flavour of the dish to which we propose to add them. Now if you were to go to a scientific conference in the food industry, you would hear learned dissertations about the tenderness, the colour and the acceptability of frozen peas, canned meats and other preserved foods. You would hear little or nothing about the nature of food flavour, the sort of flavour which is possessed by the dishes of which I am going to talk in this chapter. I by no means underrate the importance of such aspects of food quality, as the tenderness of meat and the colour of peas, but something more is needed before we can mix ingredients together to achieve the maximum possible flavour.

That something more is a knowledge of the vital interaction between the taste and the aroma of food, and this lies in the realm of the artistic cook. Cooks, in fact, are such important people that they need a section to describe the kind of skills that they require for the practice of their art.

(b) The role of the cook in the Art of Cookery

Any human skill that is not analysed and described in a textbook is generally elevated to the status of an art, as if the kind of skill that is needed is of such a specialised nature that it cannot be taught, or put into words. Cookery itself is often described as an art, although there are several specialised skills used in cookery which are well taught in the cookery schools, and it is only the knowledge of food flavour which is so neglected. I am going to list some of the skills in order to drive home the point that the tasks facing the cook must not be underestimated.

First, there is the planning of the dish, and the selection, buying and preparation of the ingredients required. Then there is the storage and keeping qualities of the ingredients, so that each is available in prime condition. After this comes the detailed preparation of the dish with the exercise of the technical skills required in chopping, sieving, mixing, thickening and homogenising, which are of vital importance if sauces are not to separate, and their appearance is to be attractive. Then, perhaps most important of all, comes the choice of the method of cooking, whether boiling, baking, frying, roasting, grilling and the like, which will best suit the nature of the ingredients to be combined into the dish. To do all these operations, the cooks of earlier centuries were trained by years of apprenticeship but I fear often with the minimum of basic learning and education. It was this which resulted in so many indifferent cooks and so few good ones. It follows that a single year or perhaps even two at a technical college is insufficient to train a good cook.

In large and important kitchens a number of cooks, who specialise in the different courses of a meal, can be employed, for it is recognised that there are very few people who can shoulder the whole burden of cooking a large and important meal. There is often a soup chef, a main course chef, a sauce chef, another for sweets and so on. In Regency times the number of cooks, each with their separate duty, sometimes ran into double figures. Consider then the task of the domestic cook, who has to be skilled in every branch of cookery, and who rarely has any assistance in the menial tasks of preparation and washing up. No wonder I have so often heard my wife sighing for a kitchen maid to do the clearing up!

To the cook's burden I shall be adding yet another skill, which is a

Season to Taste

wider and deeper knowledge of the flavour of food, and this is needed if we are to get the best out of our seasoning. It is not a difficult skill to acquire, yet in practice it would be difficult if we expected cooks to add seasonings one by one at the very time when they are preparing a meal. It is necessary, therefore, to add seasonings in the form of a previously prepared mix of seasonings, whether of herbs, seeds or spices. This was the method used by earlier generations of cooks, and in fact is still used in cookery in the form of faggots or bundles of herbs tied together, or as mixes of seasonings either enclosed in muslin sachets, or added directly to the dish. I shall be describing in detail the preparation of these seasoning mixes.

This is not a cookery book of the ordinary kind with lists of recipes from which a choice of dishes can be selected. The sauces are, however, of great importance to good cookery, and I shall therefore be including a number of recipes that illustrate this form of cookery, which I have found by experience are frequently used, and are of importance in seasoning practice. Other seasoning recipes, such as pickles, sauces and chutneys, I have incorporated in an appendix for those who are interested.

(c) The natural flavour of food

Little has been written on the flavour of food in past centuries. Dr Johnson got as far as saying that he might write a book on Cookery. This is what he said:

> "You shall see what a book of cookery I shall make! Women can spin very well but they cannot make a good book of cookery. I could write a better book on cookery than has ever yet been written; it should be a book on philosophical principles"

I doubt whether he would have written such a good book as Eustace Ude, for I am sure the latter understood the philosophy of food flavour. No one, who has read the detailed advice on the importance of meat stock in cookery, could doubt that his knowledge of flavour was supreme. He was a practical cook, and I am not diminishing his stature when I say that it was not in his power to provide a science of taste and aroma. What I am going to do, is to discuss the flavours of the five basic foods in use by man, which are meat, fish, cereals, fruit and vegetables, and set out what I have learned about their natural flavour, and how it is secreted within the food. The accent will be upon the taste and aroma of the food, which is at the very heart of food flavour and, therefore, of seasoning.

Meat Flavour

The flavour of meat is mainly derived from the juices that are contained within the cells of the meat, and which can escape when the cells are ruptured during cooking. Needless to say, the meat cells are highly complex in their nature, for example, the aqueous juices also contain albuminous matter, rather similar to the albumen or white portion of an egg, which will solidify when it reaches a certain temperature. Meat extract is a concentrate of the meat juices, and the extraction of these results in the production of a residue meat called corned meat, that still possesses a flavour, which is derived from other components of meat flavour. These are mostly aromatic in nature, and are responsible for giving meat a flavour from which the variety of meat can be recognised. For example, lamb and beef, and chicken and game each possess their own delicate aroma, and as I have pointed out elsewhere, game often has such a marked aroma of its own that seasonings are rarely added to it.

Yet another component of meat flavour is the 'sweetness', which is exemplified by the saying 'the nearer the bone the sweeter the meat', and indeed I accept the truth of this saying, for 'sweetness' used in connection with the flavour of meat, has a meaning quite distinct from the sweetness provided by sugar.

Fish Flavour

What I have said about meat flavour applies to the flavour of fish, for here again it is the juices derived from the cells that provide the desirable quality of fishiness. Fish, however, is much more perishable than meat, and the sweet flavour of a freshly caught herring, pilchard or mackerel can be quickly lost during storage. It is frustrating not to be able to describe flavour sensations more adequately in words but I hope I have been able to say enough for those interested to recognise from their own experience the quality of fishiness, or sweetness, which certain varieties of fish can possess. Alas, both fishiness and meatiness can be lost by negligently allowing the fish or the meat juices to escape during cooking, or even during the thawing of frozen meat or fish, because freezing ruptures the cells in the same way as heat. The quality of sweetness in both meat and fish, but particularly the latter, can be lost by overlong storage in a refrigerator, and the reason for this is that while the enzymes that are present in living tissue are inhibited by freezing, their activity is not stopped altogether, and the quality of freshness and sweetness is gradually destroyed over a period of time.

The flavour of Cereals
The five groups of foodstuffs were worth listing in this way if only to point out the great difference between the cereals and the other four groups. Cereals are, of course, derived from seeds, and they are dehydrated when they are ripe and ready for harvest, and they have to have moisture restored to them before they can be eaten and digested by man, although the digestive system of animals can cope with uncooked seeds.

When seeds are cooked, the starch of which they are mainly composed will take up or absorb considerable quantities of water and will, therefore, swell in size, as everyone who has made porage understands very well. Now the flavour of starch is not very marked, the flavour of the whole seed is probably derived from the non starchy parts of the seed, such as those connected with the life processes of the plant. This is a most important constituent of the seed, and in the case of wheat, for example, it can provide as much as 12 to 15 percent of protein. It is quite possible to live indefinitely on a starchy diet, as many peasants have found over the centuries.

The flavour of cereals is mostly derived from the effect of the heat of the cooking process on the grain. The classic case is bread, whose flavour is derived from baking, and slices of bread can be given additional flavour by toasting. Because of the dryness of starch, there is not the same danger of loss of flavour constituents as there is with the other foods.

The Flavour of Fruit and Vegetables
I described the changes that take place during the ripening of the orange in an earlier chapter, when the fruit acid changes gradually into sugar, and an aromatic and highly volatile oil develops in the cells, which can be quite powerful in some varieties of fruit. Much the same thing happens in vegetables, some of which, like lettuce, are very mild in flavour but others, such as the vegetable seasonings, possess an essential oil which is too strong to enable them to be eaten by themselves, so that they have to be mixed with the mild flavoured foods to reduce the strength of their flavour.

(d) Seasonings — When to use them and when not to use them

"It is but opinion, and that is the world's master alwayes"
William Rabisha in 'The whole body of Cookery Dissected' 1673

You will now appreciate what I mean when I talk about the natural flavour of food. The flavours of the basic foods can be of a very high order, and there are occasions when it is a matter of debate, whether it is desirable to add seasonings to them. Nevertheless seasonings are foods in their own right, and it is purely a matter of opinion whether they are added or not. It could be said that it is as permissible to mix basic foods and seasonings as it is to serve vegetables with meat. My personal opinion is guided by the fact that seasoning is the art of so mixing foods of all kinds together that the best possible flavour is achieved.

In deciding whether or not to add seasonings, it is essential first to consider the taste and aroma of the dish. Let me illustrate by a few examples. Consider first the seasoning of a prime quality rump steak. Now its flavour when cooked under a hot grill is so delicious that some people would say that it would be a crime to season it. There can be no question that its taste of meatiness is the most prominent feature of its flavour. It has an aroma of its own, of course, but the addition of a seasoning to reinforce its aroma, perhaps pepper or mustard, can add to rather than detract from the taste of the steak.

Next let us consider a dish of game — say grouse, pheasant or partridge. Now game differs from beef in having a much more pro-nounced aroma in addition to its quality of meatiness. In practice, our ancestors felt it was not wise to add any seasonings to this dish, and I accept their mature judgement. The reason undoubtedly is that the aroma of game is of so rare a quality that to add herbs or spices as additional aroma could only mask the excellence of its own aroma. Salt comes in a separate category and, acting only on the tongue, would not compete with the aroma of the game in any way.

Let me take some examples rather less specialised than grilled steak or game. Shall we say, a dish of beef, mutton or pork? First, the question of taste and aroma — beef must be savoury, of course, with no addition of sweet-sour ingredients. It will depend on the cut which is chosen; if it is one of those delectable carving joints, let us enjoy the undiluted flavour of the beef. So, we shall roast it and add no seasonings but I cannot enjoy beef like this to the full unless it is served with Horseradish sauce, which seems to complement the roast beef to perfection. However, suppose the joint is oxtail? This is a delicious meat but experience dictates that oxtail needs thyme, so let us choose a casserole of oxtail because the long cooking will soften the connective tissue and cause the meat to fall away from the bone, and among the seasonings for a savoury dish we shall make sure that thyme predominates. We shall consider savoury seasonings later.

Suppose, however, that we have a piece of rather old lamb in the refrigerator, showing its age by being a little fatty, let us offset the natural fattiness of mutton by treating it as a sweet-sour dish. We shall boil the mutton and skim off the fat afterwards, concentrate the stock and incorporate it into a white sauce to which we shall add a generous spoonful of capers, and season it further with some of the vinegar in which the capers were preserved, or failing that with some wine vinegar until the sauce tastes slightly tart. This is one of my favourite dishes, and I serve the mutton with the sour sauce poured over it to hide the sometimes not very attractive appearance of some mutton joints.

(e) The Rule of Natural Flavour

You will see that the decision whether or not to add seasonings to a dish depends on whether it is considered necessary to supplement any deficiency in either the taste or the aroma of the ingredients of the dish. As I am attempting to establish seasoning on a sound scientific basis, I am proposing three rules for the guidance of those who wish to add seasonings. The first rule — that of Natural Flavour — helps to establish whether or not seasonings are necessary. The rule is based on the assessment of the presence or absence of taste or aroma in the basic ingredients of a dish. Here is the first rule:

> Check the natural flavour of the ingredients of the dish, in order to assess whether or not its taste or its aroma need to be supplemented.

It is still, as William Rabisha said in 1673, a matter of personal opinion but at least it is an opinion arrived at in a rational manner. Having decided to add seasonings to a dish, the next question to be decided is which of the seasonings are to be added to achieve the maximum flavour advantage. This question I have made the subject of a second rule — the Rule of Flavour Harmony. We shall now see how this rule operates to guide the second choice that we must make.

(f) The Rule of Flavour Harmony

> Two large potatoes, passed through kitchen sieve
> Unwonted softness to the salad give;
> Of mordant mustard, give a single spoon,
> Distrust the condiment that bites so soon;
> But deem it not thou man of herbs, a fault

To add a double quantity of salt;
Three times the spoon with oil of Lucca crown,
And once with Vinegar procured from town;
True flavour needs it, and your poet begs,
The pounded yellow of two well boiled eggs;
Let onion atoms lurk within the bowl,
And scarce suspected, animate the whole;
And lastly, in the flavoured compound toss
A magic teaspoon of Anchovy Sauce;
Then, though green turtle fail, though Venison's tough,
Serenely full, the epicure may say —
Fate cannot harm me — I have dined today.

The poet's recipe for a salad. Rev Sidney Smith

If I had been sitting at the table of the well known Victorian cleric who wrote this excellent poem, who clearly would have appreciated to the full my Rule of Flavour Harmony, I am sure I would have been content to enjoy my meal without being curious about the ingredients which he used in it. If, however, I had been asked what I thought of its flavour, I would no doubt have taken the dish to pieces in my mind and would have assessed its sweetness, its sourness, or the lack of these qualities, and I would have tried to recognise the ingredients which gave it its aroma. I might have been in some difficulty however, because I am sure Sidney Smith would only have chosen such ingredients whose flavour harmonised well together. In such a case one ingredient would have blended with another so perfectly that neither would have been recognisable in its own right.

You will see what I mean when you examine the following list of dishes:

Scotch Broth or Irish Stew	meat, carrot, onion, turnip
Moussaka (Greece)	beef, onion, aubergine

Both of these dishes are mixtures of meat and vegetable, and the effect of the mixture is that an entirely different flavour has been produced from any of the ingredients tasted on their own. Some would substitute swede for the turnip but they would be wrong to do this in my opinion.

Duxelle Sauce (France)	mushroom, onion, butter, parsley

This is not a complete dish but the principle is the same, it is an excellent way of using up surplus mushrooms, and can be used as a savoury garnish with a meat dish such as a chop or a steak.

Tarama (Greece)   cod's roe, garlic, parsley
This dish demonstrates the rather unusual harmony between fish, garlic and parsley. If each ingredient is used in the correct quantity, of which more anon, the garlic, for example, cannot be detected apart from the other two ingredients.

Curry (Eastern countries)   meat, coriander, cumin, pepper,
                                     cayenne pepper, fenugreek, etc.
A curry has got to be included in a list such as this, and a good curry is a superb example of the harmony that can exist between seasonings. One must not forget the importance of the basic ingredients, however, and a curry can only be as good as the meat or perhaps the vegetables of which it is composed.

Chutney (All countries)   fruit, sugar, ginger, garlic
This is an excellent example of two seasonings, ginger and garlic, combining to produce a flavour entirely different from either of them. Chutney is a sweet condiment, as you would expect with such a spice as ginger.

Tomato Ketchup (American)   tomato, sugar, onion, cinnamon
This is a sweet-sour condiment, and rather naturally, therefore, is seasoned with cinnamon. Its high degree of popularity testifies to the harmony of the ingredients.

Gazpacho Soup (Spain)   capsicum peppers, cucumber,
                                     onion, tomato, vinegar,
                                     olive oil
This is not as well known as it might be but, even in Spain, the ingredients can be incorrectly proportioned to achieve the best flavour. I gave the recipe in the Spice chapter.

Mincemeat Tart (All countries)   dried fruits, apple, beef,
                                     sugar and cinnamon
This dates from the age of sweet-sour food and is an excellent flavour harmony.

Lasagne or Pizza Pie (Italy)   pasta, tomato, meat, cheese
Italian cookery, descended as it is from Lombard times, has excelled in the combinations it has produced from cereal, meat and cheese. The advent of the tomato from America has added a new dimension to the harmony the ingredients can produce.

Ice Cream (All countries)　　　　　　cream, sugar, vanilla

This combination must certainly find its place in any list such as this, for cream by itself can never produce such a flavour as it can when used in combination with other ingredients.

Cornish Splits (England)　　　　　　scones, strawberry jam,
　　　　　　　　　　　　　　　　　　clotted cream

This may seem an odd choice but, in fact, the combination of these ingredients provides a flavour of a very high order which is not given by any of them on their own. Cooked cereals, as is shown in cakes, tarts, pies, puddings and so on, harmonise with a great number of dishes. Add the sourness and the aroma of fruit and a still further flavour dimension is added. It is no accident that jam has been such a popular addition to bread and butter, for the same flavour harmony is at work.

These are only a cross section of the dishes which show the harmony that can exist between one ingredient and another, and one is constantly finding new examples, for example only recently I found a Canadian one, which has a rhyme to emphasise it:

Apple Pie without Cheese is like a kiss without a squeeze! I've never tried it — the dish I mean — and I mean to try it out one day!

These dishes illustrate the rule of Flavour Harmony between the ingredients of a dish, which is at the very heart of good seasoning. I am referring here to the basic ingredients of a dish. For it is these which, with the possible exception of curry, that is itself mostly made up of seasonings, give the main flavour character to the dishes I have listed. Exactly the same applies to the seasonings themselves, for are they not themselves ingredients?

There is, however, a third major requirement to achieve flavour harmony, which is the quantity of both the main ingredients and the seasonings that are to be used. I separate main ingredients and seasonings here in order to give prominence to the former, for too often not sufficient trouble is taken to achieve the best proportion of each ingredient in a dish. This can be very important in a vegetable dish, like Scotch broth or a vegetable stew, for if too much onion or carrot (both strong tasting ingredients) are used, the stew will not attain the best flavour that is possible. In just the same way, if a curry has too much cumin, which is a powerful seasoning, the curry blend will be spoilt.

This brings us to the Third Rule of Seasoning, which is concerned with the quantity of ingredients in a dish, and this applies to both main ingredients and seasonings.

(g) The Rule of Flavour Balance

"You must observe in all soups and broths that one thing does not taste more than another; but that the taste be equal, and it has a fine agreeable relish."

Hannah Glasse. THE ART OF COOKERY 1747

No book on seasoning can afford to neglect this quantitative aspect of seasoning, although few writers in the past have mentioned it. Hannah Glasse was one of the few, and the above quotation from her book is the reason she stands so high in my estimate of her abilities as a cook. Another writer, also a woman, deals with it — Eliza Acton, who published her 'Modern Cookery for Private Families' in 1845. In her general remarks in the chapter on forcemeats she says:

"No particular herb or spice should be allowed to predominate in these compositions; but the whole of the seasonings should be taken in such quantity only as will produce an agreeable savour when they are blended together".

At first sight it is rather surprising that only two cooks committed themselves to what is in effect a practical theory of seasoning, and one would have thought that more writers would have tendered advice to the family cooks for whom they were writing. The family cooks were either the mistress of the house herself or else her assistant, who did not have the advantage enjoyed by the apprentice, of the practical demonstrations by an experienced cook of the quantity of seasonings to be added to a dish. Eliza Acton had her own ideas on the subject, for she was one of the first cookery writers to give detailed advice on recipe quantities, and she included seasonings also, as is shown in the following recipe for Common Forcemeat:

Breadcrumbs 4 oz; lean of ham 2 oz; butter 2 oz; minced herbs; 1 dessertspoonful; lemon-grate 1 teaspoonful; nutmeg, mace and cayenne, together, 1 small teaspoonful; little salt; 1 whole egg, or yolks of two.

Now this was all right as far as it went but Eliza Acton must have known that she was evading the real issue in specifying 'nutmeg, mace and cayenne together, one teaspoonful'. The teaspoon is a very unreliable measure because it varies in size so much, and cayenne is a very strong spice. In another recipe she specifies the actual quantity for a Mushroom Ketchup:

"Pepper 1 oz; Allspice $\frac{1}{4}$ oz; Ginger $\frac{1}{2}$ oz; Mace 2 blades"

However, to measure a spice by fractions of a teaspoon is hardly practical. Eustace Ude was nearer the mark when he said: "—the cook on the other hand must taste often, because reduction increases the strength — it would be blind work indeed without tasting." He is quite right, of course, and in this section we are going to do just this; I am going with you into the kitchen, and I shall take you through the detailed steps in the preparation of a spice mix and a herb mix. Before I do that, there are one or two more things to be said.

You will remember that Hannah Glasse said "—that the taste be equal—", and that Eliza Acton said "—no particular spice or herb must be allowed to predominate—". They were each saying the same thing but in different words, and I must, in my turn, bring their language into the 20th century and formulate what they said in my own Third Rule of Seasoning, which I call 'The Rule of Flavour Balance'. This is how it goes:

"Check that no single ingredient of the dish can be tasted or smelt more than any other ingredient"

Now Hannah Glasse was talking about the equality of taste in soups and broths, and Eliza Acton was talking about forcemeats. They were not saying that every dish needs this treatment of equality of season- ing, for there are a number of dishes in which it is not required. Those who like the taste of clove in an apple pie, would not add another spice which could mask the taste of the clove; and those who put mustard on their beef do so because they like the taste of the mustard. The same thing applies to any dish in which it is usual for one particular seasoning to predominate. As a further example, I would cite the stuffing for a goose or a turkey where it would be unthinkable for sage not to predominate over the other seasonings.

To continue the subject of equality of taste, what we have got to consider is the type of dish, that is all too rare today, in which a balanced range of seasonings is added. What I am saying now is of the greatest importance and I beg you to pay special attention to it. When a balanced range of seasonings is added to a dish, a new flavour dimension is brought into being, in which no single ingredient can be detected and a new flavour is born. Let me illustrate this from one of the dishes in my list of flavour harmonies — the flavour of chutney, which is brought into being by the admixture of fruit, sugar, garlic and ginger.

The fruit might well be apple, and the addition of sugar has to be sufficient to convert the two basic ingredients into a pleasant sweet-sour base. Now add a small quantity of ginger until the latter can just be tasted alongside the sweetened fruit. You will be wise to heat the three ingredients in a saucepan to ensure that they are properly distributed. The next step is to add a tiny quantity of garlic. I use a small hand operated gadget that squeezes the strong tasting garlic juice a drop at a time. The first drop may not be enough to be tasted, in which case add another and a third drop until, as if by magic, another flavour begins to appear — that of chutney! You can if you wish continue the experiment by adding yet more garlic juice until the only flavour to be tasted is garlic. The flavour relationship between the ingredients can be demonstrated by a diagram thus:

Zone of Ginger   Zone of Chutney Flavour   Zone of Garlic

What we have got to find is the quantity of garlic that will produce the optimum flavour of chutney. This is a simple combination of fruit with two aromas. So far so good.

I have only cited the harmony of fruit, sugar, garlic and ginger, in order to show how two aromas can lose their own identity when they combine together, and can produce another aroma quite unlike either constitutent by themselves. I am not suggesting that seasonings have got to be added one at a time to a dish; it is theoretically possible for this to be done, as in the experiment I have just described, but it is not practically possible, for the cook is far too busy preparing a meal to have time to do so.

The logical and, in fact, the historical method of adding seasonings to a dish is to prepare a mix of the herbs, seeds or spices. This was done in the days of sweet-sour food — you will recall the Blank Powder or Lombard Powder, which were mixes of sweet spices with sugar; it is done today by mixing aromatic seeds to make a curry powder, or by mixing certain herbs into a bouquet garni. I am going to add to these mixes a savoury spice mix and a sweet herb mix which the cook can add to a dish in a single operation during its preparation. In making mixes of seasonings such as these, the rule of Flavour Balance has to be applied and I must now demonstrate how they can be made in such a way that no one aroma should predominate over another.

(h) The making and balancing of a Savoury Spice Mix

In an experiment, such as this, it is desirable to provide a mild tasting basic food, against which the spices can be tasted, and nothing fits the purpose better than a good meat stock. In a later section you will find the recipe which I use myself, that results in the making of cubes in the ice tray of a domestic refrigerator. For this exercise, we shall need a small volume measure, to measure the quantities of spices — a thimble is almost ideal, but failing this use the plastics or metal cap of a small medicine bottle. I could have specified gram weights, which I normally use, but few possess them, and the gram weights marked on spring balances are rarely accurate enough. Lastly, we shall require two small saucepans and a small quantity of the following spices — black pepper, clove, mace and pimento. These should be ground up for this experiment, and once again I refer you to a later section for the grinding of spices.

The experiment

Take three frozen stock cubes and melt them in a small saucepan. This will be our test stock. Take three further stock cubes in another saucepan to act as the unseasoned stock for comparison with the test stock. Season both stocks with an equal quantity of salt to taste. Take a level thimbleful of black pepper and add it to the test stock. Simmer it gently for a few moments and taste. Is not the flavour of black pepper exquisite and desirable?

Now take a level thimbleful of clove, simmer again and taste. Your test stock will now undoubtedly taste of clove. If this is the case, do not worry, we have yet to add the third member of the spice family — mace. This spice is so rich in oil that it tends to bind, but fill the measure, tapping it to shake it down and add it to the test stock. You may have 'gone over the top' with the clove and still be able to taste it, in which case add another measure of both pepper and mace, and then you should not be able to distinguish any spice with certainty.

When you are satisfied that you have achieved a perfect balance, taste the test stock against the unseasoned stock. Do you see now the difference between the two, and is it not delicious? I use a small quantity of pimento in my own formula, which is pepper 3 parts, clove 2 parts, mace 3 parts and pimento 1 part. I make up a quantity of the mix in these proportions, by measuring the quantities in a wine or sherry glass, and then I grind my spices in a high speed mill and store them in a glass jar with a tight fitting lid.

It might be a good idea to repeat the experiment and defer the use of black pepper until you have balanced the two spices clove and mace, each of which has such a distinctive aroma, und you may care to try nutmeg instead of mace, and perhaps try the addition of a little cardamom seed or some coriander.

The savoury spice mix can be kept ready at hand to be used when you are seasoning a sauce or a complete dish. This operation can be done using a small quantity of the mix on the tip of a teaspoon until you are satisfied with the taste. You will appreciate that this kind of mix is not suitable for a jelly or a clear soup where the ground up spices might spoil the appearance. It is more convenient to describe alternative methods of seasoning for such dishes at a later stage.

You will see that it is just as easy to prepare a sweet-sour seasoning mix by the same method, and meat stock can again be used but this time you will have to add sweetness and sourness to a stock, either by adding sugar and vinegar, or perhaps by using fruit, which will give an entirely natural balance between sweetness and sourness.

(i) The Making and Balancing of a Sweet Herb Mix
There is no essential difference between the making of a sweet herb mix and a savoury spice mix but, before I go through the drill, I think a further word must be said about the herbs we shall be using. The mix will consist of those aromatic herbs which have been found by cooks to harmonise with and enhance the flavour of savoury food. Which are the sweet herbs? I take my courage in both hands in naming them, because I know no one else in this century who has been bold enough to do so. First, the herbs about which there is no question — sweet basil, sweet marjoram, savory and thyme, and these were mentioned by Hannah Glasse as being 'sweet', that curious flavour I discussed earlier, which is something quite different from the sweetness of sugar. I see no reason to question Mrs Glasse's judgement as to these four herbs.

Then there are some other herbs, which also bear the prefix 'sweet', and chief among them is sweet bay. I have some doubt whether bay has not too distinctive an aroma to qualify it as one of the sweet herbs but then thyme also has a distinctive aroma of its own, and if it can be called a sweet herb, so can bay. The other herb, which might qualify as a sweet herb, is parsley, although I prefer to regard it as a herb which stands on its own, for it does not possess the curious but typical sweetness, or even sharpness, of the other sweet herbs. It is always difficult to use words that are adequate to describe the quality of an aroma but, though such herbs as basil, marjoram and savory have distinctive aromas of their own, they possess a mildness of aroma, in common with each other, which makes them suitable for conveying a quality of 'herbiness', which is quite different from herbs with a powerful aroma, like sage or tarragon or, even to a lesser extent, bay.

I make no apology for speaking about the relative flavours of the different herbs once again because I wish to stimulate discussion about the flavours that they possess. Lovers of wine never cease to discuss the infinite gradations of flavour between wines of different areas and vintages, and I cannot see why the same should not apply to the herbs.

For making a sweet herb mix, we shall need the same things we used with the spice mix, that is to say, six frozen stock cubes, two small saucepans and a supply of the four sweet herbs — thyme, basil, savory and marjoram. I shall assume that you will not have these herbs growing in the garden as I have, and we shall, therefore, use the commercial dried herbs one buys from the supermarket but do buy fresh supplies from a reputable manufacturer if your stock is more than, say, three months old.

The Experiment
Take three frozen stock cubes and melt them in a saucepan — this is the test stock. Now take three further cubes in another saucepan to compare with the test stock. As in the spice experiment, season both stocks with the same quantity of salt. Now take a thimbleful of dried parsley — tap the thimble to obtain a levelfill, and add to the test stock. Simmer it for a few moments and taste, observing the kind of flavour that parsley can provide. Next, add half a thimbleful of thyme and taste again. Whether or not you can taste the thyme will depend on the freshness of your herb but you should be able to taste it in this concentration. Now add a thimbleful of basil, and follow it with an equal quantity of sweet marjoram and then savory. It is not a bad idea to leave the stock for a few minutes, in order to rest your palate. When you return, taste the unseasoned stock and then the test stock. Which herb can you taste? If one stands out above the others you will know that it must be reduced on your next attempt. If your herbs are reasonably fresh, you will find out just what a sweet herb mix can do to add flavour to savoury food — a delicious sweet herbiness like a summer garden after a shower of rain! As with the spice you can make up a convenient quantity for use in your cooking.

(j) The freshness of Herbs, Seeds and Spices

For the sake of simplicity, I have assumed that a spice or a herb mix will be made from dried herbs and dried spices. Now, as spices are imported from distant countries, they have to be dried as soon as they are harvested, and it is a common sight in the spice growing areas of the world to see such spices as pepper or clove or ginger spread out on mats or sacks to dry in the hot tropical sun. This is not very different from cereal grains, which have to be harvested when the grain has dried to a point that it can be safely stored for long periods of time, although in moist climates grain dryers are often necessary to reduce the moisture content artificially. Herbs, however, can be used in both the fresh and the dry condition, and unfortunately the act of drying them tends to damage the leaf structure and cause a serious loss of the aromatic oils, on which herbs rely for their flavour. Let me explain just what happens when a herb is dried.

When an aromatic herb is fresh, all its volatile oil and its natural moisture is contained within the substance of the leaf. The art of drying it lies in retaining the volatile oil, and thus its flavour, while aiding the gradual escape of its moisture. It is important to avoid damaging the structure of the leaf, which would allow both the essential oil and the moisture to escape. Unfortunately, the leaves are easily damaged when they are stripped from the stems on which they grow, and some herb leaves are so securely attached that it is quite difficult to release them. I will describe the method which I use a little later.

Now the important question — is there a difference between the flavour of fresh and dried herbs? The answer must be yes, because however careful we are, the leaves must suffer some damage in drying and stripping, and there must be some loss of the essential oil. I believe there is some loss of flavour too, in the sense that fresh herbs have a fresher taste and, when dried herbs are more than a few months old, they tend to acquire what I describe as a 'dried grass' flavour, and seem to retain little of their original aroma. Alas, many of the dried herbs which are contained in the attractive bottles that decorate many western kitchens, have acquired the 'dried grass' flavour and are fit for nothing but the dustbin. Using them can do no good to the good name of herb cookery, and we badly need a supply of herbs of guaranteed freshness.

Herbs in northern lattitudes are planted in the spring and harvested in July to September. Now these 'new seasons' herbs have to work their way through the manufacturing process, and can hardly be on sale until October at the earliest, so that any herbs purchased in, say, September must be at least a year old by that time. In practice, many of the herbs in our kitchens are many months old, so that it is quite possible that a proportion of them are at least two years old by the time they are used. Now with many preserved foods there will be little if any loss of flavour but remember that herbs are highly aromatic in their nature and, with the processing hazards I have described, they are greatly at risk. I have found, by experience, that it is wise to change one's stock of herbs annually, and in the absence of any statement about the age of the product, the only really effective way of obtaining herbs of good quality is to grow them yourself.

It is not a very accurate test of freshness but all one can do when buying herbs is to take a pinch of them between finger and thumb, and then smell the result. There ought to be a quite pronounced smell of the herb concerned.

(k) The growing and drying of Seasoning herbs
There are so many excellent books these days on the raising of plants in the garden that I would not dream of claiming that my method is superior to any other and the only points I shall mention are those which I have found important. I grow only those herbs which my wife and I use in our day-to-day cooking, about a dozen varieties in all — parsley, thyme, sweet marjoram, sweet basil, winter savory, sage, chives, French tarragon (not the Russian variety which has no flavour), mint and bay. To these must be added a few which I grow for the sake of curiosity and general interest.

I have a small glasshouse in which I raise my seeds in the early spring, planting them out into a herb bed when the weather is warm enough. The basil is rather an exception because it dislikes the cool English summers, and as this herb is my favourite, I transplant it into the garden frame which gives it some protection against the inclement weather. The rest I find do well enough to provide me with fresh herbs from June to October, and to meet my needs for dried herbs for the rest of the winter. Parsley likes both sun and a little shade, and my rose garden seems to give it what it likes. I cover it with a cloche during the winter and it generally lasts into the spring. Thyme, bay and savory, being perennials, give a year round supply, and I sometimes wish the other sweet herbs were perennial too. Pot marjoram is a perennial plant but most people who have grown it think it is not as good as sweet marjoram. Basil, however, is the king among herbs, and I measure my success or failure by the growing of this lovely herb.

When autumn comes, and before the various plants become too woody, I carefully cut my crop of the various herbs, and spread them on a frame covered with plastics net, which I hang in the roof of my garage. This works quite well provided the door is left open, and they are protected from sun or light, which can cause discoloration. The herbs will wilt but it is sometimes quite difficult in this damp and cool English climate to extract all the residual moisture from them, and this is particularly the case with a herb such as basil, which has a tough and rather leathery leaf when it is dry. Some artificial heat is often necessary to complete the drying, and this may be done in a domestic oven, provided that a temperature not above 120°F is used. In my oven I turn the thermostat to its lowest setting and this gives me the desired temperature. If the temperature exceeds 120°, there is a danger of losing the volatile oils, and an excessive drying temperature can easily be the cause of the poor quality of some of the commercially dried herbs. Packing of the herbs into sealed plastics bags completes the operation.

The next operation is stripping the leaves from the stems, and I do this by agitating the plastics bags to try to get as many leaves as possible detached from their stems. Herbs will vary a great deal in this respect, and one has to do the best that one can to detach the leaves without damaging them. Sometimes I have used a little wheeled cutter to chop them, for, although the cutting of the leaf damages them, the greater part of the leaf remains undamaged. This may seem rather laborious in comparison with the purchase of a packet of commercial herbs but I wish I could say that these compared favourably with the home produced product. Alas, even as a manufacturer, I have to admit that the latter is greatly superior to the former.

(l) Seeds and spices — Whole or Ground?

> "Gregory Young's Pepper to be new garbelled and returned to him, and G.C.'s Cloves in like manner."
> THE RECORDS OF THE GROCER'S COMPANY. Dec 1571

This quotation shows that our ancestors were well aware of the variability in the quality of spices. The Wardens of the Worshipful Company of Grocers were given legal powers to control the spice trade, and protected the public by inspecting the stocks held by merchants, and either ordered his stocks to be destroyed, or to be 'garbelled'. Garbelling was sieving and, in the 16th century, the City of London had a chief Garbeller, who was a progenitor of our modern food inspector. The following extract from the records of the Company tells its own story.

"John Rogers Wormsede was viewed — he did not send in the remnant of Cloves according as the wardens appointed him. Then the wardens showed such powders, dust of spices and olde and naughty drugges that judgement might be given upon the same. First, Richard Denman's powder of Ginger was viewed and found that it was deceiptfully mingled with such things as were not convenyent, and therefore judged worthy to be brent—."

Fortunately for us, the modern food inspector looks after our interests, and when we buy cloves or ginger there is little danger of them being adulterated — "with things that are not convenyent"!

What we want to know more about is the relative strength of the spices we buy, that is to say, the whole spices compared with those already ground for our use. I was perhaps guilty of oversimplification when I was describing the differences between herbs and spices in an earlier chapter. For the sake of clarity I did not then disclose that, in addition to an essential oil, which is common to all three classes of the vegetable seasonings, each of them also has in addition an oleoresin constituent, which is resistant to loss by evaporation. As I mentioned earlier, each spice, in addition to its essential oil and its oleoresin, has a third constituent, a naturally occurring chemical. The result is that the spices are not dependent solely on their essential oil for their aroma, and therefore they will not lose their flavour as easily as either herbs or aromatic seeds. Another reason, of course, is that the essential oil is better protected than is the case with herbs. Nevertheless, spices do lose flavour once they have been ground, for once their protective covering has been fractured, the essential oil must evaporate.

The aromatic seeds also keep their flavour very well until their horny shell is broken, and then there is little to prevent their essential oils from disappearing. I mentioned this in connection with curry, when describing the aromatic seeds, and the desirability of grinding or crushing the whole seed in preparing a curry powder. I never buy ground seeds or spices unless I am forced to do so by lack of the whole seasonings.

It is now desirable that we should return to our herb and spice mixes, in order to see just what happens when we add them to our dishes. The chief actor here is water, and this may seem rather strange until we realise what an active ingredient it becomes in our saucepans.

(m) The role of water in cooking

Water is such a familiar ingredient in our food that we tend to take it for granted, yet whichever method of cooking we use, whether boiling, roasting, baking and so on, it is water that is naturally present in food, or that we add to it when we cook it, which is responsible for many of the physical changes in the food that affect its flavour.

Water is the highly mobile carrier of the aromatic substances we use in seasoning; it is responsible for mixing one flavour with another, and an understanding of its role will assist us in ensuring that it works for us instead of against us. Up until now we have only had to pay passing attention to it but now we can neglect it no longer.

Imagine the varied activity when, for example, an Irish Stew is cooking. Imagine the stew in a saucepan gently boiling on a gas ring. The water it contains is boiling and conveying heat to all the ingredients. It breaks down the meat cells, releases the gravy they contain, suffuses through the meat, softening the muscle tissue, dissolving it and carrying it into the stock. The boiling water is absorbed by the potato and its starch swells, it softens the carrot and the onion, it melts the fat from the meat by breaking down the connective tissue that holds it to the meat and to the bone. In the process of doing all this, it becomes enriched with the soluble constituents from the meat and the vegetables, and acquires a delicious flavour, a flavour that is enhanced by the seasonings we have used in the dish.

Now we all know that at sea level water boils at 100°C and, when it is coming to the boil, the molecules, of which water is composed, become more and more active, until when the water boils they reach a frenzied state of activity — bombarding the solid ingredients with which they come into contact, and most important of all, bombarding the surface of the water in the saucepan and escaping into the atmosphere as steam. The steam is no longer water but a gas, and it will carry with it other gases, such as the volatile aromas which the dish contains. That is the reason why the aroma of Irish Stew is carried all over the house! The effect of this on the seasonings is clear. They are first bombarded by the water molecules and their aromas are extracted, and if the boiling is too severe the steam will carry the aroma away and it is lost.

If you place a sprig of thyme in a saucepan of boiling water, the smell of the thyme will quickly fill the kitchen. Continue to boil for a very few minutes, and there will be no aroma remaining; it will all have evaporated into the air. Now for something you will find in few, if any, textbooks. If the dish in which you place the thyme is not water but is of a fairly thick consistency, and most important of all, if a little fat is present in the dish, then the volatile oil of thyme will dissolve in the fat, with which it has a great affinity, and this will materially delay its evaporation into the atmosphere. I have noticed this effect very frequently, and I think it can be put down to the much higher boiling point of the fat. Naturally, at the boiling point of water, the 'loose' fat in the dish will be in the form of oil. The volatile oil of the seasoning will have secured for itself a haven, as it were, in which it is no longer being bombarded by the active water molecules, and it will be, to a great extent, protected from their attack.

I always look upon the fat or oil in a dish as a very useful means of 'carrying' the volatile oils of the seasonings, and a French cook of the last century A. Beauvilliers, in his 'L'Art de Cusenier' of 1814, said:

"I have learned by experience that of all the fats that are used for frying, that which is taken from the surface of the broth and stock pot is by far the best."

This is not surprising because it contains all the aromatic qualities of the dish, and it teaches a valuable lesson, that while the aqueous portion of the stock is required for one kind of dish, the fat that comes from it is equally valuable for another. On the other hand, there is no virtue in excessive quantities of fat or oil in a dish. Just the reverse in fact, because then we get fatty and oily tastes, which are often objectionable. I have found that the only time when quite a lot of fat or oil is permissible is when it is required to produce a smooth texture such as occurs in cream. In the ordinary way only sufficient fat should be used to perform its essential purpose in a dish. A good example is the serving of one of those soups with a few small rings of oil floating on its surface, just sufficient to carry the aromas of the soup.

(n) Extracting the flavour from herbs, seeds and spices
In the light of what we now know of the action of water in the cooking pot, we can appreciate what happens in the four classic ways in which we can extract the aroma from the vegetable seasonings. Here they are:

Season to Taste

Method I

The seasonings can be ground up, or pounded in a stone or wooden mortar, as was done in times past, and the resulting mix, or as much of it as was desirable, was added directly to the dish. This is the straightforward way of adding them, and probably the most widely used. Its only drawback is the presence of small bits and pieces of the seasonings, which might impair the appearance of the dish. The curry seeds are added in this way, and the appearance of the ground seeds is a characteristic feature of the curry.

Method II

The seasonings, whether ground up or not, can be sewn or tied up in little muslin bags or sachets, which can be placed in the saucepan or cooking pot, and removed before the dish is served. It is not so necessary to grind the spices in this method because their flavour will be transferred to the dish during the cooking process. Seeds on the other hand should be crushed before cooking because of the toughness of the shells which enclose them.

Method III

The seasonings can be tied up with string or cotton into a bundle or faggot which is immersed in the cooking pot, in just the same way as the muslin sachet. Eustace Ude and countless other Regency cooks used to include with their bundle of herbs a blade or two of mace and two or three cloves wedged under the tightly tied string. This was then called a 'seasoned' faggot.

Method IV

The unground seasonings can be added just as they are to a dish in the course of preparation, and allowed to soak overnight in the liquor in which the main ingredients of the dish are to be cooked later. This is called a Marinade, and it is a very simple and effective way of transferring the aromas to the dish. The seasonings are sieved off before the start of cooking. This process can be speeded up by simmering the seasonings in the liquor for a short time. This variation is useful if one has not had time to marinade the ingredients overnight.

It can be seen that the choice of method depends not only on the nature of the dish but on whether or not ground-up herbs or spices are to be used. It must be realised that the presence of, for example, specks of black pepper may be permissible in a domestic household but they are quite out of the question in a restaurant or a hotel. As we have not had many recipes so far in this section, it may be useful to give the recipe for a Bechamel sauce by Mrs Young, until recently the proprietor of a fishing hotel on the shores of Loch Awe in Scotland.

Mrs Young's Bechamel Sauce
Ingredients
 Milk ½ pint, one bayleaf, one blade of mace, peppercorns, onion stuck with one clove, one carrot sliced, flour ¾ oz, butter ¾ oz.

Method
 Put the herbs and spices, onion and carrot in a pan with the milk, cover and leave on low heat to infuse. In another pan melt the butter, add the flour and cook for a minute or two (this is of course a white Roux). Draw off the heat and add the strained milk by degrees, stirring all the time to avoid lumps. Return to the heat and still stirring, bring to the boil and allow to boil for a few minutes to thicken.

This recipe uses method 4 outlined above, and the removal of the spices is a perfectly simple operation of sieving them off with the carrot and the onion.

Having said that this is perfectly simple, as indeed it is, there still remains a pressing need for an easier and more efficient way of using vegetable seasonings than we have at present. The operations which are involved are often tedious, consisting as they do of tying herbs up into bunches, or herbs and spices in muslin bags, and I believe something better should be available in the latter half of the 20th century. We want the aroma and taste of the seasonings but we do not want the woody and inedible fibrous residues which accompany them. We want the true and natural seasoning packaged in such a way that its aroma is preserved in fresh condition for a reasonable period of time.

There is something else that we want even more urgently, and that is a measured quantity of the seasoning, that we can add directly to our dish during its preparation, which will take the guesswork out of seasoning. It is simply not good enough that the only measure we have at home is the humble teaspoon which, even if it did not vary in size, is normally much too large a quantity for the domestic dish. Having been a food manufacturer, I know that what I request is reasonable, for several specialist firms, who supply excellent products without any of the woody residues, exist. What remains to be done is to package them into a suitable form for use by the domestic cook. I feel sure that one day we shall wonder how we ever managed to do without seasoning pills which contain all the advantages but none of the drawbacks of the natural article.

(o) Gravy

"It is on a good first Broth and Sauce that you must depend for good cookery."

Eustace Ude. THE FRENCH COOK 1813

This quotation shows how important were the gravy and the sauce to a competent cook in the 19th century, and, while the gravy was served quite unseasoned, the seasonings were mostly incorporated in the sauce. It is necessary, therefore, that we look carefully at these vital adjuncts to savoury cooking, and their relationship to the meat broths and stocks that were constituents of them.

We saw that it was the introduction of the iron cooking stove in the 17th century that made it possible for small iron saucepans, with flat bottoms, to be heated on the stove, and this produced a revolution in cookery. The meat, fish and vegetables could all be accommodated in separate vessels, their juices saved, seasoned and served separately as gravies and sauces.

Gravy is the thin and very appetising liquid that drips out of a joint of meat while it is being cooked. When a large joint of beef is roasted, the gravy, which is really the juices from its underdone centre, will seep through the outer layers of the joint and forms a pool in the roasting pan, from where it can be collected and used either for basting or for serving a small portion to moisten each serving of beef as it is carved. The gravy only oozes out when the joint is underdone because, when the meat is fully cooked, the meat albumen in the gravy coagulates or sets just as the white of egg coagulates when the egg is boiled. The juice is then trapped in the centre of the joint, or if the fire is very hot, evaporates on the surface of the meat to form that rich brown and flavoursome crust one gets when a steak is grilled. I mention these points only to show how different is a gravy from the stock we shall consider in a minute. It is interesting that in the 18th century meat gravy was served in elegant little jugs fitted with very thin spouts to limit the quantity of precious gravy. These jugs were called Argyles.

The quantity of gravy was always limited by the size of the joint, and cooks have always realised the advantage of buying meat specially suited to supplement the meatiness of a dish, and in practice it is usual to extract the meat juices by means of boiling water, to produce the good 'First Broth' of Eustace Ude's quotation. This is so important that it deserves a section to itself.

(p) Meat Stock

This was Eustace Ude's description of the recipe which was the foundation of all his cookery.

First Broth

Take part of the breast, or rump of beef with some of the trimmings, and put the meat into a stockpot with cold water. Set it on the fire, and watch the proper moment to skim it well. If this broth be not clear and bright, the other broths and sauces are sure to be spoiled. Be particular in taking off the black scum; then pour a little cold water into the broth to raise up the white scum. When all the scum has been removed, put in a few carrots, turnips, heads of celery and leeks, four large onions, one of which is to be stuck with five Cloves; and throw a handful of salt into the stockpot and let the whole simmer for five hours. Skim away the fat, then strain the Broth through a double silk sieve. Lay the piece of beef in a brazier pan; pour over it some of the broth to keep it hot, till the moment it is served. Broth is made in this manner, when the beef is wanted to be used for one of the removes; otherwise cut the beef smaller, to be sooner done. This first Broth will serve to moisten all the other broths, of which the different names are as follows—.

The other broths were First Consommé or Stock Broth, Consommé or Stock Broth of Poultry, Consommé of Game, Stock Broth or Rabbits, Blond of Veal and so on. Common to all these stocks was some of the First Consommé or Stock Broth made from the First Stock described above. All very confusing, but it fitted the pattern of cookery and dining in large houses, clubs and restaurants. If one had inspected the large coal fired stove in the average kitchen in the morning, it would have boiling on it a number of stockpots, all ready for making the number of sauces required for a meal. They are not suitable for today's cookery, which is on a much simpler scale in the average household, and I shall now describe just what Ude and other cooks of his time were doing, and the type of product they were obtaining.

Meat stock is different from gravy by reason of the fact that it is made by simmering the meat in gravy or water. While the gravy from the meat will exude into the water, the latter will also react with the collagen or muscle tissue of the meat and will convert it at least part of the way into gelatin. This process we call hydrolysis. Stock, therefore, is a mixture of gravy and the gelatinous product produced by the action of hot water on meat. The stockmaking process has always been rather mysterious, and I think few people really understand the full significance of the resulting product. I have done quite extensive research on the subject, and this is what I have found.

For all practical purposes, there are two elements in a meat stock. The first and obvious element is the quality of meatiness in itself, which is flavour of a very high order. I have never heard a vegetarian explain away the fundamental fact of the existence of meat flavour, and while I accept that nuts have an excellent flavour of their own, they do not and cannot taste of meat. Meat flavour originates in the cells of which red meat is composed. Blood may be red in colour but it does not contain meat flavour.

The other element of stock is the gelatinous thickness, which is produced by the process of hydrolysis. It has no real flavour in itself other than the meatiness, which may be present, that is derived from the cells of any red meat used in the stockmaking process. The cook may be deceived into thinking that this relatively flavourless stock can be of little flavour value. This is very far from being the case, and my main contribution to the science of meat stocks is the recognition that a gelatinous stock has the property of modifying and improving the flavour of other ingredients used in a dish. This can be illustrated by a simple experiment.

Dissolve a commercial stock cube in half a pint of water. Now take a similar cube and dissolve it in a stock made by boiling bones in water. When you compare the two stocks, you will find that the one containing the bone stock has a much better and more rounded flavour. It is difficult to understand just why this is so, seeing that the bone stock of itself makes no contribution to meatiness but I believe that the gelatine of the stock coats the surface of the tongue, and modifies the response of the taste buds to other flavours that are present.

There is one other ingredient which I have found improves the flavour of a meat stock and that is the addition of a marrow bone cut so that the marrow inside the bone is exposed to the action of the hot water. There are certain chemical reasons that could be adduced to explain the flavour improving quality of beef marrow but these lie outside the scope of this book.

The effect of adding meat stock to a dish, quite apart from the flavour advantage bestowed by the additional meatiness, is that it seems to blend the flavours of all the ingredients together, and make a dish which is made with stock better than one which is made without it. While a modern commercial stock cube can convey a certain stimulated meatiness to a dish, it lacks the one essential ingredient — which is the gelatinous stock that modifies the response of the taste buds to other flavours. It is the product of an ingenious mind. It contains hydrolysed yeast protein, and vegetable extract and sodium glutamate, and even sometimes contains some meat extract as well but not very much of this because it is very expensive. Although, as I have said, it adds a certain simulated meatiness to a dish, it lacks the one ingredient which can make a stock such a useful product — it does not contain meat stock!

So important is meat stock to the flavour of a dish, and because there are so many ways of making it, I have listed the various kinds of meat stock in descending order of merit. Here they are:

A. The ideal meat stock is prepared from raw meat and a marrow bone, cut so that the marrow it contains is exposed during extraction.
B. Failing the marrow bone, not quite so good is a stock with raw meat only as one of the ingredients.
C. Failing both raw meat and a marrow bone, next is a stock made with muscle tissue such as bones and skin or sinews.
D. Then comes, about level pegging with C, the average commercial stock cube but without the blending effect of the viscous stock.

There is nothing I need add to the above other than to say that it is not necessary to buy the most expensive cuts of meat to obtain the benefits of a good stock. Some of the best stocks can be made from the necks of animals. This applies to lamb, chickens and other meats, and, as for game, the whole carcasses are a rare prize for the making of game soup, surely one of the most delectable gastronomic treats!

It goes almost without saying that manufacturers should produce a stock cube which really is a stock cube, for it is easier for this to be done in a properly equipped factory than in a domestic kitchen. I would not expect the manufacturer to go to the expense of using the flesh of meat, because of its high cost, and this surely can be added by the user if the cost is thought to be justified in a particular dish. What the factory can provide is the stock made from a suitable muscle tissue as well, perhaps, as bone marrow, thereby saving the user a great deal of toil and trouble.

Because the real thing is not, as far as I am aware, available, I shall give my own recipe for making the frozen stock cubes I prepare for my own use; these are suitable for almost any dish. The only seasoning which I use is parsley supplemented with bacon and onion but these can, of course, be omitted when they are not required. I give the recipe in detail in order to explain the reason for the individual steps in the process.

Frozen Meat Stock Cubes

The cubes can be made in the icetray of any good refrigerator, and when they have been frozen I keep them in a plastics bag until required.

Ingredients

Shin beef or chicken necks or the equivalent	2 lb
Streaky bacon rashers	4 oz
Onions	one large or two small
Chopped parsley	1 tablespoonful
Marrow bone	Only the centre part containing the marrow

Method	Technical reason
1. Place bacon in bottom of saucepan.	To ensure that loose fat is rendered down.
2. Cut the meat in chunks of about 1 in. size and place in saucepan.	This enables the meat juices to escape into the stock.
3. Place marrow bone among the meat pieces and add parsley.	This ensures that the marrow will be melted out of the bone.
4. Add onion, cut in pieces, and water (cold) to cover all the ingredients.	This will 'hydrolise' muscle fibres and produce an equal volume of solids to liquid.
5. Bring to the boil very slowly — about half an hour.	Slow heating will give clearer stock. See below.
6. Simmer, but do not boil for 3-4 hours.	Rapid boiling will break up the meat albumen and cause cloudiness of the stock.

The slow heating will assist the trapping of cloudy particles escaping from the meat, and this is important if a clear jelly stock is required. Care should be taken in pouring off the stock from the solids left in the stockpot, to avoid cloudiness in the stock. This stock can be skimmed to remove fat on the surface, or else can be cooled overnight and then easily removed. Finally, warm to melt the stock sufficiently to pour it into the ice tray of a refrigerator for freezing.

You will be left with solid pieces of meat, which you may think it a pity to waste, and these can be added to a stew or a similar product. Do not expect much flavour from them, because it has been largely removed but the meat will have shrunk because of the cooking it has received, with the rather odd result that its calorific value will be higher than when the meat was raw! All of which goes to show that the flavour of meat lies in its soluble constituents. A word must be said about the other flavour constituents of meat. Meat is a complex biological substance and, while meatiness is its main flavour constituent, it is by no means the only one. Each kind of meat carries its own flavour, beef, mutton, lamb, pork and so on. It is my experience that the flavours which characterise any particular meat seem to reside more in the solid meat and bone than they do in its soluble meat constituents. This is particularly marked in game.

(q) The Sauce

We must now look at the interesting subject of the sauce which is served with savoury dishes, and with sweet-sour dishes too, for there are a number of sauces that contain vinegar or sour fruits, which take them out of the savoury category. I remarked elsewhere that it was perfectly legitimate for sour sauces, such as Worcester sauce or Tomato Ketchup, to be served with savoury food, for the palate craves for a sweet-sour sensation to counterbalance the 'neutrality' of so much of the food which contains no sour constituents. Ude makes clear that he depended on the broth and on sauce as the most important elements in his cookery, and they are the natural carriers of the seasonings, which gives them great importance to us. Most cookery books of Regency days paid great attention to them, and the chef who founded the firm with whom I spent all my working life — W. H. Brand — devoted a whole chapter of his book 'The Complete Modern Cook' to the sauce, no less than sixty separate sauces being listed.

A sauce by no means always contains meat, although it is difficult to find one which does not contain an admixture of meat stock in one form or another. In contradistinction to gravy, which is always thin, a sauce is always thickened in some way, and this makes a sauce not only useful as a masking agent or a garnish but gives it an attractive appearance in itself. The thickness may be derived from a puree of vegetables, or from an emulsion of vinegar, oil and egg, as in a mayonnaise, or from an emulsion of butterfat and milk, us in the case of cream, or simply from flour or starch.

I propose in this section to give some examples of different types of sauce, with particular reference first to their seasoning and secondly to the manner in which they can be emulsified. Science can help us considerably in these days in the matter of forming and stabilising emulsions of oil or fat and water, and for that matter it can help us to understand the effect of flour and starch on emulsions. For this reason, I shall start by describing the roux-making process, which is of the greatest use in cookery, and will serve as an essential introduction on modern advanced techniques of sauce-making.

The Roux

Roux is a French word derived from 'russet', the colour which is characteristic when flour and butter are heated together. Place an ounce of butter in a saucepan and warm to melt it, and then add an ounce of flour. When the pan is heated gently and the mixture stirred with a wooden spoon, it starts to bubble and fizz as moisture from the butter and flour is driven off as steam. As soon as the moisture has evaporated, the roux takes on a smoother shinier appearance and begins to darken in colour or 'caramelise' as the temperature rises, which is the same change as takes place when the crust of a loaf darkens. What is actually happening as we stir the mixture is that the fat is being broken up into tiny globules as the flour is being stirred into it. At the same time the protein is being 'denatured' by the heat, and it acts as an emulsifying agent, as it were, suspending and stabilising the globules of fat, and it is this which gives the smooth shiny appearance.

If the fat-flour mixture is mixed for a very short time we get what is known as a white roux. If it is heated rather longer we get a blond roux, and if the heating is continued longer still we reach the stage when it is called a brown roux. The white roux is used for the making of white sauces of the Bechamel type, while the darker roux is used for Brown or Spanish sauces.

Whichever colour is used, the final stage in the roux process is reached with the addition of water, and when this happens the change is dramatic — the water is rapidly absorbed by the roux and it swells in size and quickly reaches a stage when no further water is required for the starch swelling process. Sometimes the butterfat can separate at this stage, and this depends on the efficiency of the stirring while the water is being added. In normal circumstances, however, the swollen starch will still maintain the globules of butter in suspension.

The roux-making process is important, and performs two functions. The first is the suspension of the butter globules in the starch thickened sauce but the second is almost more important, for it is producing to the desired extent a caramelised flavour by the browning of wheat flour, a process analogous to the baking or toasting of bread. When the water addition is replaced with stock, one can appreciate that two flavour elements are at work and a base is provided for the display of a number of different seasoning combinations. This is the point to describe my Madeira sauce recipe, which makes full use of the roux-making process.

Madeira Sauce
Ingredients
  Flour (plain) $1\frac{1}{4}$ oz
  Butter $1\frac{1}{2}$ oz
  Beef stock   8 oz (as frozen cubes)
  One small onion
  2 mushrooms for garnish
  1 sherry glass of rich Bual Madeira wine
  Savoury Spice Mix to taste
This recipe is seasoned with savoury spices and with Madeira wine. Herbs are omitted because I believe two groups of seasonings are sufficient; herbs being a third group would have been overdoing the seasoning.

Method
  Melt the butter in a saucepan over low heat and add the flour, stirring as in the roux-making process until a brown roux is produced. If it is taken too far, bitterness may result. Melt the required number of stock cubes in a saucepan and add the onion peeled and sliced. Simmer for a few minutes until the onion is cooked. Strain off the onion and add your savoury spice mix on the tip of a teaspoon until you judge, by taste, you have added sufficient. Make up the volume lost by evaporation and add to the roux,

stirring well, and add salt to taste. Return to the heat and add the mushrooms sliced thinly to display their shape, bring to the boil and simmer for a few minutes. Finally, add the Madeira wine and serve.

The next sauce is going to be made by an entirely different process, in order to illustrate the other and more modern way of making a flour-butter emulsion. As the sauce is to be a Sauce Supreme, a white sauce, we do not need to use the roux-making process, for reasons that will appear.

Sauce Supreme
First with regard to the name — Supreme Sauce. The nomenclature of sauces in the various countries is quite an involved subject, in which I do not wish to get involved. The French would claim that this is a 'sauce composée' having more ingredients than the basic flour, butter and milk of a basic sauce known as a Bechamel or a Velouté. For my purposes, Supreme is a white sauce, which can be served with a number of dishes, and I wish to concentrate on the technological aspects of the sauce and, of course, its seasoning.

Ingredients
    Chicken stock 8 oz. Flour 1 oz. Butter 1 oz. Skim milk powder.
    1 level tablespoonful, 1 sliced carrot, 1 onion.
    Seasonings — Salt to taste,
                Herbs — a faggot of sweet herbs
                Spices — 6 white peppercorns, 1 blade of mace and
                        2 cloves.

Method
    Melt the stock cubes in a saucepan, and add the carrot and onion cut in slices, and the three spices, bring to the boil and simmer for a few minutes. Melt the butter and place it in a high speed mixer with the flour, the milk powder and the seasoned stock, after the vegetables and spices have been sieved off. Mix at high speed for from 3 to 5 minutes.

This will produce a fine emulsion of the butter and the meat stock, with the flour and the milk powder acting as a stabiliser of the emulsion. Liquid milk could have been used.

Pour the emulsion into a saucepan and heat to boiling, stirring constantly. Season with salt to taste and add a faggot of Sweet Herbs, using thyme, winter savory, sweet marjoram and basil, with a bayleaf, if desired.

This sauce will stand up to any normal cooking process without separation and can be served with any dish which requires a thick sauce of delicious flavour. The stock can be made from chicken necks, giblets or chicken carcasses, which can be obtained at very reasonable cost. Sauce Supreme provides a very convenient starting point for what I want to say on Creams and Creaming, which deserve a separate heading.

(r) Creams and Creaming

I want to talk here about the physical nature of creams and not about the flavour of cream as such, because I discussed this in an earlier chapter. Now dairy cream is an emulsion of butterfat and milk, which can be stable at quite a wide range of levels of butterfat. In the United Kingdom there is a regulation that cream must contain 48 percent of butterfat to enable it to be sold as Double Cream; 18 percent butterfat can be called Single Cream; and a minimum of 38 percent qualifies as Whipping Cream.

If one looks at a drop of dairy cream under the microscope, it can be seen that it consists of a myriad of tiny droplets of fat floating in a watery liquid. If you were to shake the cream vigorously after adding some water to it, the fat droplets would gradually collide with each other and, after a time, the emulsion would break down into its constituents — butter and milk. When Hannah Glasse in the 18th century was making her Chicken Fricassée, she advised that the cream should be stirred 'all one way', and this was to avoid needless agitation and collision between the butterfat droplets, which would cause the separation or breakdown of the cream into its constituents.

Now an emulsion between fat or oil and water requires just the right conditions to remain stable without separation into its constituents, and it may be helpful if I detail some of the precautions that have to be taken in cookery to achieve a stable emulsion. Science and technology can be quite helpful because we now have a better understanding of the forces that are at work and which affect stability. As this knowledge does not seem to be widely known, the following comments may prove useful, and these apply as much to dairy cream as they do to an artificially made cream of vegetable oil or animal fat.

Firstly, the proportions between the fat and the water must be within a certain safety range. If the water or the fat phase of the cream is too high, then the bonds between the minute globules of fat and water will be too weak to maintain stability. We have already seen from what Hannah Glasse said that rapid agitation of an emulsion can cause its breakdown, by causing the fat droplets to overcome the forces that bind them together, and allow them to separate. Another factor is the size of the droplets, and an emulsion will be more stable if they are finely emulsified. In the recipe for Supreme Sauce, I specified a high speed mixing time of from 3 to 5 minutes to ensure that the droplets were reduced fairly quickly, although this does depend on the speed and power of the mixer.

The most important factor of all is the presence of a third ingredient, known as an emulsifier, which is most commonly a protein. Most proteins will act by, as it were, anchoring themselves in both the fat and the water droplets, and acting as a bond between the two phases. This, I fear, is not a very scientific explanation of the action of an emulsifying agent but it is nevertheless broadly speaking a correct one. Milk provides the protein which ensures the stability of dairy cream, and you will notice that I used it in the recipe for Supreme Sauce for this purpose. I find by experiment that about one percent by weight of skim milk powder will achieve the desired result. Egg provides the protein which is the emulsifying agent for mayonnaise but here the oil content is often so high that the egg yolk has the greatest difficulty in ensuring the stability of the mayonnaise. Generally, the oil is added a small amount at a time, to ensure that it is broken up finely. Here is a recipe for a mayonnaise which is taken from Larousse Gastronomique.

Mayonnaise Sauce II (Old recipe)
Put into a medium-sized bowl 2 fresh egg yolks, a little salt and white Pepper and a little Tarragon vinegar. Stir this mixture quickly with a wooden spoon. As soon as it begins to thicken, blend in, little by little, a spoonful of Aix Olive oil and a little vinegar, taking care to beat the sauce against the sides of the bowl.

On this continued beating depends the whiteness of the mayonnaise. As it takes on more body, add more oil, a little more vinegar and, at the beginning, a little aspic jelly. It is essential to put these ingredients in a little at a time, to prevent curdling.

You will need for this preparation 2 cups of oil, half a cup of aspic jelly and enough Tarragon vinegar to give an appetising taste. To make it whiter, add Lemon Juice.

(A. Careme, L'Art de la Cuisine Française)

You will notice that the stability of the mayonnaise is assisted by the use of a little gelatin to provide thickness. You will see also that adequate beating is necessary to achieve whiteness. In fact, the colour of a cream is a fairly reliable measure of the fineness of an emulsion. The smaller the droplets of oil and water, the whiter the emulsion will be. It is characteristic of a cream that, being of a very dense whiteness, it is quite difficult to colour it by the addition of another colour. This is an optical effect and is due to the fineness of the droplets dispersing the light falling upon them.

This brings me to the last point I wish to make about creams and creaming, for what we are really attempting to do is to provide smoothness of texture, and this can be done by raising the oil content to a point where the desired physical creaminess is achieved. A mayonnaise is a very specialised type of sauce with its very high oil content, much higher than is ever needed for general cooking purposes. I have found that there is rarely any need to go above the 50 percent fat content of dairy cream but even this is much too high for most vegetable oil emulsions. Quite a good creaminess can be provided by an oil or fat content of 10 percent, without running the risk of a taste of fattiness when too high a content is used. We have already seen that a very small quantity of fat is all that is necessary to 'carry' the essential oils of the seasonings in a dish.

(s) Final Reflections
Seasoning is no more and no less difficult than cooking. Either can be very plain and simple, or highly evolved and complicated. It is the art of mixing foods together to obtain good flavour. This is the first book, I believe, to be written to show scientifically how this can be done, and I trust that this aim has been achieved.

There is much interest today in the use of herbs and spices, for people feel that the pendulum has swung too far and that it is time we started to have a change from 'the meat and two veg' of Victorian days. We have a wonderful array of native herbs, and we still have the spices from tropical countries to add variety to our food, although I fear we have largely forgotten how to use them. The use of herbs and spices is an art in the sense that the way we use them depends on our personal judgment of what constitutes good flavour. History shows, however, that there is a good consensus as to how they should be used to obtain the maximum flavour from our dishes.

What can herbs, seeds and spices do for food flavour? When used in the way I have suggested, they can add a wholly new dimension to food flavour, and the art of adding them can be learnt in the same way as the art of painting is learnt. Seasonings can be used sparingly or generously, in just the same way as paint can be applied thickly or thinly to a canvas. Science, however, can be of great assistance to the cook in a number of ways, and none of them is more important than the modern knowledge of taste and smell.

Of all the advice that I have given, one piece of advice stands above all the others — do not forget that everything depends on the natural flavour of food, and that no seasoning can improve the flavour of poor or badly cooked food. It was because the Victorians did not realise this basic fact that seasoning fell into disrepute, and only now are herbs and spices beginning to return to our tables. Finally, I salute the cooks of all ages from the great Roman Apicius to Gervase Markham in the 17th century, and from Hannah Wolley in the 17th century to Eustace Ude in the 19th century. They were great artists in the manipulation of food and I revere their memory and am deeply grateful to them for all they have taught me.

Seasonings and Condiments

HERB RECIPES
   Sweet Herbs
   Bouquet Garni
   Turtle Herbs
AROMATIC SEED RECIPES
   Curry Powders
   Comfits
   Scotch Comfits
   Cardamom Coffee
SPICE RECIPES
   Sweet Spice Powders
   Savoury Spice Mix with herbs
   Paté seasoning
   West Indian Cocktail
SAUCE RECIPES
   Poivrade Sauce, W. H. Brand
   Bechamel Sauce, Mrs Young
   Anchovy Sauce, E. S. Dallas
   Quin's Sauce, unknown
   Reading Sauce, unknown
PICKLE RECIPES
   Cashmere Chutney, W. H. Brand
   Fine Mushroom Ketchup, E. Acton
   Mustard Pickle, the author
   Pickled Mushrooms, Elizabeth Raper

Seasonings and Condiments

There are a number of recipes for seasoning combinations, as well as condiments, such as pickles and sauces, which need to be recorded for the use of students of seasoning. It has been difficult to choose those which are worthy of record out of the large number which are available, and inevitably I have had to use my own judgement on which it is best to use in order to give a balanced view of our subject: For ease of reference, I have arranged them so that recipes for herbs, and those for aromatic seeds, spices and the sour seasonings are grouped together, and I have included certain recipes at the end which are just too good to leave out.

Herb Recipes
The first recipe is my own formulation of Hannah Glasse's Sweet Herbs which is as follows:

Sweet Herbs
Sweet Marjoram	2 parts
Winter Savory	2 parts
Sweet Basil	2 parts
Thyme	1 part

You will no doubt vary the mix to suit your own taste, and in any event, when the opportunity occurs, you really must compare fresh and dried herbs, so that you can appreciate the great difference between them.

Next comes Bouquet Garni: a number of formulae are available, one from Elizabeth David is the same as my own Sweet Herbs Mix but the more usual recipe, which is also recorded by her, is as follows:

Bouquet Garni
    2 whole Bay leaves
    A sprig or two of dried Thyme
    A few fresh Parsley stalks

For certain dishes, such as Doubes of Beef, she adds a strip of orange peel and a piece of celery.

One of the most useful books on herb formulae is Milo Miloradovich's 'The Art of Cooking with Herbs and Spices', which gives a goodly number of recipes for the experimental cook. However, the large number of possible combinations makes it impossible to list them, and all I wish to say is that a distinction should be made between the mild herbs, such as those which constitute the Sweet Herb mix, and the powerful herbs, which must include onions, garlic, tarragon, mint and sage. The mild ones can be used freely and with little limitation but the powerful ones must be used with discretion because they can so easily swamp and overpower their weaker brethren. The Fines Herbes combination is only another name for Bouquet Garni, with the important exception of the Fines Herbes combination used by Brand, of onion, mushroom and parsley, which was described in the 'Age of Elegance' chapter.

Next must come Turtle Herbs, which represent a highly specialised use of herbs. As I have recorded elsewhere, I do not know who originated this most interesting herb combination. Few writers detail them and the one I use is that of Simpson, who makes the only mention I know of the unusual Orange Thyme* but, having grown it in my garden, I cannot detect any flavour of orange.

Turtle Herbs, dried
    Take Basil, Pot Marjoram, Orange Thyme, Lemon Thyme, and Common Thyme, Parsley four times the quantity of the other herbs; put them to dry gradually (so as to take four or five days to dry) when quite dry, rub them with the hand through a hair sieve; then put them in a cannister, or a bottle, and keep in a dry place, they will be found very useful for seasoning forced meat and many of her purposes, and not the smallest expense. They will keep good for years.

I am afraid I just don't believe John Simpson, when he says that his dried herbs will keep good for years, as it is against all one's experi-

*Its botanical name is Thymus Azoricus.

ence but he has clearly got a new idea in the recipe for Turtle Herbs in glaze.

Turtle Herbs in Glaze

Take Marjoram of both sorts an equal quantity, half the quantity of Basil, four times as much of Parsley; Lemon, Orange and Common Thyme the same quantity as Marjoram, all picked from the stalks; to a large handful of each herb put one pound of Shalot, two pottles of Mushrooms, chopped very fine, two pounds of lean ham, a few truffles, if to be had, as they help the flavour; put into a stewpan one pound of butter, one quart of the best stock, and then the herbs, ham, etc. Put the stewpan on a slow stove to stew very gently for three or four hours, or until the stock is quite reduced, and the herbs and ham quite tender; then rub them through a tammy; then put them into a stewpan, add one quart of glaze made from the best stock, or the bottom of braises, put them on a quick stove, and keep stirring them while on the fire, which should be until the glaze is reduced one quarter, or until the herbs become quite thick, and begin to stick to the bottom of the stewpan: then put it into oval or round potting pots, as they are more handy than deep preserving pots for cutting out small quantities; those herbs will retain their flavour for six years, or longer. I have had them by me for that length of time, and found them equal in goodness to the first day. Turtle herbs done in this manner will be found very useful for Mock Turtle, Calves Head Hash, matelot of different kinds of fish; it takes but a small quantity to give the proper flavour to the above mentioned uses, about a quarter of an ounce to a pint of sauce, and so on to a larger quantity. NB They would be found very useful to take to the West Indies.

Another herb combination is Ravigote, well described in Kettner's 'Book of the Table'. The French give the name Ravigote to an assemblage of four herbs tarragon, chervil, chives and burnet. They are minced finely or used as a faggot and are supposed by their fine flavour to have the rare faculty of resuscitation. Ravigote Butter contains these chopped herbs and salt, pepper and lemon juice are added to it. Ravigote Sauce is a butter sauce to which a Ravigote is added.

Aromatic Seed Recipes

Pride of place must, of course, be given to the Curry recipe. Here are five recipes from my collection, which for ease of comparison, I have set out as a table.

Curries

Ingredient	Dr Hunter's (Indian Curry Powder)	Dr Arnotts (ex Eliza Acton)	H. W. Brand (No. 2)	H. W. Brand (No. 3)	Recipe X2 (author)
Coriander Seed	4 oz	4 oz	22 oz	8 oz	6 parts
Cumin seed	—	2 oz	6 oz	2 oz	1 part
Turmeric	4½ oz	8 oz	8 oz	8 oz	1 part
Fenugreek Seed	—	2 oz	—	6 oz	1 part
Mustard Seed	1½ oz	—	—	—	2 parts
Cardamom Seed	1 oz	—	—	1 oz	—
Cayenne Pepper	1½ oz	½ oz	1 oz	1 oz	½ a part
Black Pepper	3 oz	—	10 oz	8 oz	—
Pimento	—	—	4 oz	—	—
Cloves	½ oz	—	1 oz	—	—
Cinnamon	—	—	6 oz	—	—
Ginger	½ oz	—	4 oz	4 oz	2 parts
Mace	½ oz	—	—	—	—

In my view the two obligatory ingredients of a curry are coriander and cumin. Turmeric and paprika are used for the colour they provide, and fenugreek, mustard and cardamom are usual. On the other hand, cinnamon is rather unusual, and I do not think that a curry is either sweet or sour enough for this spice to taste at its best.

The savoury spices pepper, nutmeg or mace, clove and pimento, and the aromatic seed cardamom, can all be used but these are not, in my view, a fundamental part of the curry formula, and should be used as a savoury spice mix to give a general savoury flavour to the dish to which one is to add the curry powder. The correct method of their use is, therefore, to add the savoury spice mix to the basic ingredients of your dish, and only after this to add your chosen curry powder, until the desired strength of curry is reached.

Another stage still could be the addition of the desired amount of Cayenne pepper, for this is very much a matter of personal taste. I use very little cayenne because I believe it tends to mask the aroma of the other curry ingredients, although I am prepared to admit that an Indian who lives in a hot country would be unlikely to agree with me.

Comfits

It was the 17th Century which saw the great flowering of the dessert or pudding course of the meal, and many cook books contain sections on what we would now call confectionery recipes. One of the most interesting confections was the sugared Comfit, which featured the aromatic seeds, although John Murrell has recipes not only for anise and caraway but also others for candying nutmegs, ginger, oranges and lemons. He also has a recipe for Muscadines or Kissing Comfits, and these are made by the simple method of incorporating the flavour of the aromatic seed in a sugar icing paste, which is rolled out and cut into diamond shapes. The recipes which I am going to give have clearer directions, and I take them from D. Hughson's 'New Family Receipt Book' of 1817.

The Art of Making Caraway Comfits

In order to facilitate the making of comfits, a confectioner's copper preserving-pan should be provided, with two handles, and proper rings or pieces of iron at each side, for the admission of hooks fastened at the ends of a cord. This cord, or rope, being put round a pulley fixed to a beam, and the hooks thus connected with the pan, it swings at the slightest touch, and enables the operation to be more readily performed. With a little management, however, such shifts may be made, with other culinary vessels, as will nearly as well answer the purpose. The pan, then, being in readiness, and the caraway seeds cleansed or sifted, so as to be entirely free from dust, some common syrup must be boiled in a saucepan, for about a quarter of an hour; and then have the finest white starch, just dissolved or softened in cold water, mixed with it. In the meantime, some gum arabic, dissolved likewise in water, must be made slightly warm in another saucepan; and the pan, slung as described or as nearly similar as can be contrived, is to have a charcoal fire beneath it, placed at the bottom of a large tub, so as to receive but a gentle heat. When all is ready, and the bottom of the swinging pan just warm, the caraway seeds are to be put in, a ladleful of the gum water immediately added, and the seeds briskly stirred and rubbed with the hands till they feel dry; a ladleful of the starch syrup is then to be thrown in, and stirred in the same manner till dry. The process must be more or less repeated according to the size or goodness of the comfits; and, indeed, the proportions of sugar and starch will be governed by these objects. In very common comfits there is scarcely any sugar in the first coatings, and not much in the last, but best comfits, on the contrary, have but little starch, even at first, and the syrup is boiled higher for the last coats. The gum may be used for only three or four coatings, and then the starch and sugar. After seven or eight coatings and dryings they are to be set in the stove and, next day, undergo a like process. This is to be daily pursued, till they are of the requisite size; which, for the largest and best sorts, is sometimes repeated five or six successive days but the common caraway comfits may easily be finished at once.

Scotch Comfits

These, which may be considered as among the largest and best sorts of caraway comfits, must not only be gradually and well coated with rich syrup but should have a quantity of rose or orange flower water introduced both with the starch and gum solutions.

Finally, there is a paragraph which deals with the colouring of Sugar Plums and Comfits, that contains information which was new to me "that when a beautiful red colour is needed, five grains of cochineal, boiled with half a drachm of cream of tartar in a teacupful of water for about twenty minutes, with the addition of a bit of alum, not larger than a pin's head, will be at once exquisitely rich, and very wholesome. "Is this, I wonder, worth the attention of technologists who strive to attain a red colour of natural origin?

A recipe I have never tried is that for Cardamom Coffee, an Abu Dhabian delicacy. I include it because it is the only recipe I know in which the sole flavouring is that of the aromatic seed cardamon — with the exception of course of cardamom comfits themselves.

Cardamom Coffee

Qahwa, the coffee of all true Abu Dhabians, is a joy in itself. It is the colour of a clear cedar lake and its aroma clears the head; its flavour sweetens the breath. It soothes the nerves and is good for the digestion.

You can make it with four teaspoonsful of coffee beans, one tablespoonful of cardamons and a quart of water. Roast the beans to golden colour by stirring in a skillet and grind them to a fine powder. Grind the cardamons coarsely, bring the water to the boil in a saucepan, add the ground coffee and continue boiling for five minutes.

Put it aside to settle and pour coffee on the cardamom. Serve from a flask clockwise in small cups without handles. Guests drink from the same cup; just pass it around, pouring half cupsful to be sure there will be enough.

Spice Recipes

There are numerous recipes for mixtures of spices and by no means all of them are properly balanced, with the result that when you make them up you may find that one or other of the constituents can be

Season to Taste

tasted above the flavour of the others; one should never be able to taste one more than another. You must remember that there are basically two kinds of spice mix, or at most three if one includes sweet-sour food, one for sweet and the other for savoury dishes. A mix which is suitable for cakes is unsuitable for savoury meat dishes. Several of the recipes for sweet spice mixes have come down to us from early recipe books — three in fact are known to me. They are usually mixed with a considerable quantity of sugar, which is quite natural, as this served to dilute the spices and secure their even distribution in a dish.

Sweet Spice Powders

	T. Cogan 1612	The Goodman Powder 1390	The Duke's Powder 1390 for Hippocras
Ginger	10	20	39
Cinnamon	5	4.5	15
Grains of Paradise	—	2.3	39
Nutmeg and Galingale	—	—	7
Sugar	85	73	—
	100	100	100

I have adjusted the recipes to the same total, to help with comparison, and it can be seen that their main difference is between Ginger and Cinnamon. It will be seen that there is no sugar in the Duke's powder, because the wine itself would be expected to provide its own sweetness. There is of course no reason why additional sugar should not be added if more sweetness is desired. I use the Duke's powder for making Hippocras spiced wine, and having made up a quantity of the spice mix, I use a heaped teaspoonful of the ground spice powder to each bottle of wine — a sweet Muscat one. I shake the bottle each day for about four house, and then let the spices settle for another two days, before carefully decanting the wine into a clean bottle. You will, I fear, be unable to obtain Grains of Paradise, unless an enterprising merchant decides to import some from Nigeria, and cardamom seed can be substituted for it.

Savoury Spice Mix
For the sake of completeness I give here the formula of the mix, the

making and balancing of which I described earlier. While this suits my own taste, others may well see fit to vary the proportions to suit themselves.

Black Pepper	3 parts
Mace or Nutmeg	3 parts
Clove	2 parts
Pimento	1 part

Herbaceous Mixture

Brand used an herbaceous mixture in his meat cookery, which combined both spices and herbs, and this was the formula he used:

clove	2 oz	basil	1 oz
mace	1 oz	marjoram	1 oz
cayenne pepper	¼ oz	thyme	1 oz
nutmeg	2 oz	bay leaf	1 oz
white pepper	½ oz		

Personally, I think his clove is rather high, at any rate for my own taste.

It was usual in Edwardian times and before, to use a more elaborate spice mix for cooked meat dishes such as patés, boars head or brawns and ham and veal pies. A spice mix such as the above was suitable. It is necessary to grind the whole spices and enclose them in a muslin bag so that the finely ground seasonings can be used to season the stock which is added to the solid meat, and so that specks consisting of ground spices cannot find their way into the product. I make up a spice mix of the separate spices and grind them in a high speed coffee mill, using perhaps a dessertspoonful of the mix in my sachet.

In the making of a cooked meat product it is not permissible to use a plain gelatin solution to fill the spaces between the pieces of meat. Doing this results in a flavourless paté or pie, which one so often meets with in commerce today. Those who do this lose a golden opportunity of adding positive flavour to the dish in the form of a meat stock which is seasoned with one of the savoury spice mixes.

A cooked meat spice mix I use myself does not use herbs as part of the formula because I prefer to have my separate herb mix to use when I think it necessary. It does use Juniper berries, which seem to add a rather special aroma to the dish.

White Pepper, Coriander, Mace, Ginger — 7 parts

Pimento (Allspice) — 4 parts

Juniper berries and Clove — each 2 parts

The spices are mixed and ground, and kept in a sealed jar to be used a dessertspoon at a time in a muslin bag for seasoning meat stocks.

A West Indian Cocktail

Lastly, a spice recipe I came across in Grenada, which uses one of the chief exports of the island, Nutmeg, as a seasoning.

Lime Juice	1 part
Water	5 parts
Sugar	2 parts } as a syrup previously prepared
Rum	3 parts
Augostura Bitters	A few drops
Lemon	A squeeze in each glass
Nutmeg	A generous sprinkling of grated nutmeg in each glass

The Cocktail is served cold with ice.

Sauce Recipes

The 18th and 19th centuries saw the introduction of the sweet-sour sauce, which was often made at home and called a store sauce, and at a later time was produced by the food manufacturer. As I have said elsewhere, there is great scope for such sauces to be served with savoury food, for such food often requires the sharpness of a separately served sauce for the full appreciation of its flavour.

The first recipe is for Poivrade Sauce and Larousse says of this sauce that its characteristic is its peppery taste blending with that of the various vegetables and aromatics, sharpened with vinegar. I am using H. W. Brand's recipe for it:

Poivrade Sauce

Reduce a little white vinegar with a few sprigs of Tarragon, a few Pepper corns, an eschalot and a little ham: When the sauce is nearly reduced, add seven or eight spoonfuls of a Velouté Sauce and a little Consommé. Stir until boiling. Let it simmer till the sauce is well flavoured. Strain it through a tammy into a small stewpan. Add a little Cayenne and Lemon Juice if it is not sharp enough.

Bechamel Sauce

This is the recipe used by Mrs Young, the wife of the proprietor of a fishing hotel on the shores of Loch Awe in Scotland:

½ pt milk	Onion stuck with one clove
Bay leaf	1 Carrot, sliced
Mace	¾ oz Flour
Pepper corns	¾ oz Butter

Method

Put the herbs and spices, onion and carrot in a pan with the milk, cover and leave on low heat to infuse. In another pan melt the butter, add the flour and cook for a minute or two. Draw off the heat and add the strained milk by degrees, stirring all the time to avoid lumps. Return to the heat and, still stirring, bring to the boil and allow to boil for a few minutes to thicken.

You will notice that only the flavour of the carrot and onion as well as that of the seasonings was required, and it was a simple matter to strain off onion, carrot and seasonings before adding their flavour, diffused in the milk, to the butter-flour mixture. The use of the onion to carry the tiny dried flower buds of the clove is of ancient origin and I mentioned it earlier.

Anchovy Essence or Sauce has a very long and honourable pedigree, going back, probably, to Roman times. E. S. Dallas, the author of Kettner's Book of the Table, also held this belief. Do not forget that the anchovy is one of the really useful ingredients that can be used in Savoury Cooking. Hannah Glasse used it together with the oyster to add flavour to some of her dishes. Here, for example, is the seasoning of a forced meat she used in stuffing a rolled rump of beef; 'a little pepper, an anchovy, a nutmeg grated, a little Thyme, a good deal of Parsley, a few mushrooms . . .'

The recipe for Anchovy Essence I have taken from Dallas's Book:

Anchovy Sauce

The essence of Anchovy sold in shops is so often adulterated that it is wise to know how to be independent of it. Clean six anchovies and pound them in a mortar with a tablespoon of Capers, two shallots and two red Chillies. Put them in a small stewpan with Thyme, Bay leaf, Mace and a wineglassful of Mushroom Ketchup, and let them simmer gently for five minutes. Then add two wineglassfuls of good broth and reduce it rapidly. Press it through a sieve, and finish it with a small piece of glaze and a little lemon juice. Never mind the want of colour, which in the essence in the shops is too often the result of baneful minerals.

The red coloration of the anchovy is an indication that it has developed its mature flavour in the salt in which it is packed, yet when the fish is washed free of salt and ground up finely, the colour is a rather unattractive grey. The colouring used in my day was simple iron oxide, which was harmless enough, but in some countries the use of such colour is banned altogether.

Season to Taste

Pickle Recipes

The manufactured sauces of today have their origins in a number of named sauces of early Victorian days. One of these is Quin's sauce. Who Quin was I never knew but here is the recipe for his sauce:

Quin's Sauce
   4 bottles of Port Wine
   4 bottles of Walnut Pickle
   3 lb of Anchovies
   1 lb of Shallots
   1 quart of Soy
   $1\frac{1}{4}$ oz of Cayenne Pepper
   1 gallon of Mushroom Ketchup

Reading Sauce
   9 lb Anchovies
   9 gallons Soy
   $4\frac{1}{2}$ gallons Mushroom Ketchup
   2 lb of Chillies
   $2\frac{1}{2}$ lb of Garlic

Both these sauces are based mainly on the ketchups of walnut and mushroom and would have been very dark brown in colour but an earlier ancestor of the thick fruit sauces is Cabul Sauce, which H. W. Brand dated as 1843. The main ingredients of this sauce were apple pulp, raisins and Cashmere chutney, and it is too complicated to be given here but the formula for Cashmere chutney is worth giving because it illustrates a chutney recipe which certainly should find a place in this book.

Cashmere Chutney

Raw Garlic	$\frac{1}{2}$ lb
Coarse Lisbon Sugar	2 lb
Sultana Raisins	$1\frac{1}{2}$ lb
Jamaica Ginger (green)	2 lb
Cooked sour Apple Pulp	4 lb
Salt	$\frac{3}{4}$ lb
Chillies	$\frac{3}{4}$ lb
Vinegar	4 pints

As I mentioned elsewhere, the obligatory seasonings of a chutney are ginger and garlic, and the main ingredient is fruit. Undoubtedly, the finest flavour is given by a highly aromatic fruit, such us the mango, but the apple can itself possess a fine flavour, assisted in this case by sultanas. Chutneys are usually sweet rather than sour, and therefore favour the use of vinegar as the most important seasoning. In my own opinion, the four pints of vinegar are excessive in the recipe, and the keeping qualities of the chutney are best secured by an increase in the sugar content. Vinegar would only be used normally in order to supplement the natural sourness of the fruit.

Tomato Ketchup has come into popular favour, to such an extent in these days, as to overshadow the original Ketchups, of which the most important was Mushroom.

There is no need for a recipe for Tomato Ketchup, because the manufacturers, aided as they are by modern technology, provide such excellent products. But Mushroom Ketchup is worthy of being better known. There are a number of recipes available and I have chosen that of Eliza Acton and added some technological advice regarding her recipe.

Fine Mushroom Ketchup

Mushrooms	2 gallons
Salt	¾ lb to each quart of liquor
Pepper (black)	½ oz to each quart of liquor
Mace	1 drachm (3-4 grams)

One of the best and most useful of store sauces is good home-made Mushroom Catsup, which imparts an agreeable flavour to any soup or sauce, and at the same time heightens the colour without imparting the 'bitter sweetness' of browning. The Catsup ought, in fact, to be rather the pure essence of mushrooms, made with so much salt only as is required to preserve it for a year or longer.

Break up small, into a deep earthen pan, two gallons of large ripe mushroom flaps, and strew amongst them three quarters of a pound of salt, reserving the larger portion of it for the top. Let them remain three or four days, and stir them gently with a wooden spoon often during that time, then turn them into a saucepan, heat them slowly, simmer them for fifteen to twenty minutes. Strain the liquor closely from them without pressure; strain and measure it; put it into a clean saucepan, and boil it quickly until it is reduced by half. For every quart allow half an ounce of black peppercorns and a drachm of mace (3 to 4 grams).

It is at this point I must take over from Eliza Acton, and warn anyone who desires to follow this recipe that, in a sauce of this kind, there is a risk that deterioration may set in, as the salt content may not be sufficient to preserve it. Our modern means of preserving are, however, much more reliable than those that were available to her, and I am going to substitute my own suggestions, for the correct bottling procedure, to replace the very unreliable ones that she gave. The point of boiling down the Catsup to reduce its volume by half is, firstly, to increase the strength of the salt which is the preserving agent. My bottling suggestions are as follows:

Use bottles of the standard ketchup-type, which are fitted with a modern closure and a plastics insert. If new ones are not available, old bottles can be used if they are carefully washed and, together with the caps, sterilised by boiling in water. The Mushroom Catsup should be filled when as near boiling as possible into the hot bottles and immediately screw on the caps tightly, and invert the bottles to sterilise the internal parts of the cap and the neck space.

Once the cap has been removed, organisms can gain access, and the keeping qualities of the Catsup cannot be guaranteed.

Pickle Recipes

Pickles can be divided into three categories according to their relative sweetness or sourness. As the sweet end of the scale we have chutneys, which are mostly preserved by their own sweetness together with the natural sourness of the fruit from which they are made. At the sour end of the scale we have sour pickles with very little sugar and they derive their keeping qualities from the vinegar alone. In between, there are the sweet sour pickles, of which I gave an example in the text. The following is a recipe for a Mustard Pickle, or rather just the sauce for such a pickle, for the vegetables are merely onion, cauliflower and gherkin, which can be purchased already prepared in vinegar:

Mustard Pickle
  Batch size 2270 grams
Ingredients

Ginger	57 grams
White Pepper	38 grams
Mustard	95 grams
Turmeric	38 grams
Coriander	19 grams
Mace	5 grams
Cloves	5 grams

Season to Taste

Chillies	2.5 grams
Bay Leaves	2.5 grams
Garlic	38 grams
Shallot	113 grams
Pimento	38 grams
Brown Vinegar	1900 grams

Mustard is the most important seasoning and there are a number of varieties of mustard seed, some of which are hot to the taste, and others possess more of the distinctive aroma of mustard. One of the latter varieties should be used in Mustard Pickle, and the specialised advice of a blender of mustard should be sought.

The other sour pickle is that of Elizabeth Raper, who wrote her recipe for pickled Mushrooms between 1756 and 1770.

To Pickle Mushrooms

Take the buttons, rub them with a clean dry cloth, the open ones to be peeled, and the gills taken out, put them into a saucepan with a little salt, and over a slow fire, when they boil let them boil pretty fast for 5 or 6 minutes, until they feel tough. Then strain them out (save the liquor) and lay them in a clean cloth covered over till dry. Put them in your glasses. Take the best Vinegar, not too sharp, a little Mace, a few Cloves, some White Pepper, Nutmeg and a Race of Ginger, and put to the vinegar with the liquor the mushrooms were stewed in, and boil them all together for a few minutes. When cold, put this pickle into the glasses over the Mushrooms enough to cover them.

I have left this recipe just as it was and if you decide to try it, you must modernise it yourself as Elizabeth Raper leaves several points in doubt. The mushrooms she used would have been field mushrooms and a pickle recipe such as this would have been a most useful way of providing oneself with mushrooms, which would normally only have been available in quantity towards the end of the summer, when the ground was warm enough to favour their growth. There is some point in her advice to peel these mushrooms, because they might otherwise have carried an infection into the pickle. The reason for removing the gills, I believe to be that it is otherwise almost impossible to dry the mushrooms after washing them, and a dry mushroom was necessary to ensure keeping qualities.

Bibliography

Part I

Anthimus.   De Observatione Ciborum 5th century.

Bailey, W.   Pepper — A Short Discourse. 1588.

Benjamin and Castle.   British Flora Medica.

Bryene, Dame Alice de.   The Household Roll of 1412.

Buee, W. V.   The Cultivation of the Clove Tree. 1797.

Clair, Colin.   Of Herbs and Spices. 1961.

David, Elizabeth.   Spices, Salt and Aromatics in the English Kitchen.

Day, Hervey.   The Book of Curries.

Genders, Roy.   A Book of Aromatics. 1977.

Hoechstettarus, J. P.   De Cinnamone. 1670.

Husson, C.   Etude sur les Epices. 1883.

Larousse Gastronomique.

Laws Grocers Manual. ed. W. G. Copsey.

Leicester, Countess of.   The Household Roll. 1265.

Lewis.   Introduction to Pharmacology.

Lio-tio-Fane, Madeline.   The Odyssey of Pierre Poivre Mauritius and the Spice Trade 1958.

Loewenfeld, Claire.   Herb Gardening 1964.

Mackaile.   Macis Macerata 1677.

Mason, Charlotte.   The Lady's Assistant. 1775.

Miller, J. Innes.   The Spice Trade of the Roman Empire. 1969.

Miloradovich, M.   The Art of Cooking with Herbs and Spices.

Moncrieff, R. W.   Odours.

Muller, A.   Columella on Agriculture.

The Northmen.   Columbus and Cabot.

Nourse, Timothy.   Campania Foelix. 1700.
Parry, John W.   Spices. 1969.
Pliny.   Naturalis Historiae.
Redgrave.   Spices and Condiments. 1933.
Ridley, Henry.   Spices. 1912.
Rohde, E. S.   A Garden of Herbs.
Smith, Canon Sydney.   Poet's Recipe for a Salad.

Part II
Acton, Eliza.   Modern Cooking for Private Families. 1846.
Albert, S. M.   Albert the Great. 1948.
Ancient Church Orders.   Cambridge Liturgical Handbooks.
Apicius, De Re Conquinaria.   4th Century.
Aresty, Esther B.   The Delectable Past. 1965.
Austin, Thomas.   Two Fifteenth Century Cookery Books. 1888.
Barber, Richard.   Cooking and Recipes from Rome to the Rennais-
    sance. 1973.
Bartolomeus Anglicus.   Mediaeval Lore. 1905.
Beeton, Isabella.   Household Management. 1861.
Bingham.   Antiquities of the Christian Church. 1840.
Brand, H. W.   The Complete Modern Cook. 1834.
Brillat Savarin.   Transcendental Gastronomy. 1884.
Le Calendrier des Bergiers. Paris 1493.
Cambrensis, Giraldus.   The Historical Works of.
Challamel, Augustin.   Memoirs de Peuple Fransise 1866-73.
Charlemagne by H. A. Lamb. 1852.
Chaucer.   The Canterbury Tales.
Clair, Colin.   Kitchen and Table. 1964.
Cogan, Sir Thomas.   The Haven of Health. 1584.
Coryat's Crudities. 1611.
Dallas, E. S.   Kettner's Book of the Table. 1877.
Dictionaire d'Archeologie Chrétienne.
Drew, K. F.   Notes on Lombard Institutions. 1956.
Easton, S. G.   The Era of Charlemagne. 1961.
Encyclopaedia of Christian Ethics. 1912.
English Church Homilies. 1562.
Englishwoman's Domestic Magazine 1836-1840.
Evelyn, John.   Acetaria — A Discourse on Sallets. 1699.
Flower and Rosenbaum.   The Roman Cookery Book. 1958.
The Forme of Cury. 1390.

Foulke, W. D.   The History of the Langobards. 1907.

Francatelli, Chas.   The Modern Cook. 1845.

Gigault de la Bedollière.   Histoire des Moeurs et Vie Privée des Français 1847-49.

Glasse, Hannah.   The Art of Cookery. 1747.

The Goodman of Paris. Translated by Eileen Power. 1928.*

Guy, Christian.   Une Histoire de la Cuisine Française. 1962.

Hall, Thomas.   The Queen's Royal Cookery. 1713.

The Harleian Manuscripts. The British Library.

Hazlitt, W. C.   Old Cookery Books. 1886.

Harrison, Molly.   The Kitchen in History. 1972.

Hughson, D.   The New Family Receipt Book. 1817.

Juvenalis, D. J.   Satyrographi Opus Interprete. 1523.

Kettilby, Mary.   A Collection of above 300 recipes. 1724.

Kitchener, Dr William.   The Cook's Oracle. 1817.

Latham, Jean.   The Pleasure of your Company. 1972.

La Varenne.   Cusenier François. 1653.

Lebault, Armand.   Le Table at la Repas à travers les siècles. 1873.

Le Grand d'Aussy.   La Vie Privée des Français.

Lindsay, Seymour.   Iron and Brass Implements of the English House. 1964.

Maclean, A. J.   Fasting and Abstinence. 1932.

Maclean, A. J.   Ancient Church Orders. 1910.

Manfredi.   Opera Nuova il perche Venetia. 1526.

Markham, Gervase.   The English Housewife. 1631.

May, Robert.   The Accomplish'd Cook. 1660.

Menagier de Paris (The Goodman of Paris). 1393.

Mollard, John.   The Art of Cookery. 1801.

Mombert, J. I.   History of Charles the Great. 1888.

Moxon, Elizabeth.   English Housewifery. 1749.

Messisbugo, C di.   Compositione de Vivande. Ferrara 1549.

Murrell, John.   Two books of cookerie and carving. 1617.

Napier, Mrs Alexander.   A Noble Boke off Cookry (translation) 1882.

Oxford Dictionary of the Christian Church. 1961.

The Parker Society. General Index.

Pichon, J.   Le Menagier de Paris. 1846.

Pisanelli, B.   Trattato de Cibi. Roma 1583.

*See also Menagier de Paris and Pichon.

Piton, C.   Les Lombards en France. 1892.
Platina, Baptiste de.   De Honesta Voluptate. Ferrara 1475.
Pullar, Phillipa.   Consuming Passions. 1970.
Rabisha, William.   The Whole Body of Cookery Dissected. 1661.
Raffald, Elizabeth.   The Experienced Housekeeper. 1769.
Raper, Elizabeth.   The Receipt Book of. 1756-70.
Rose, Giles.   The Compleat Cook. 1682.
Rundell, Mrs M. E.   The New Family Receipt Book. 1810.
Scappi, B. Opera de M. B. Scappi.   Venetia 1570.
Simpson, John.   A Complete System of Cookery. 1806.
Smith, Eliza.   The Compleate Housewife. 1728.
Solera, I. I Lombardos.   An Opera. 1846.
Spain, Nancy.   Mrs Beeton and her Husband. 1948.
Stucki, J. W.   Antiquitatum Convivialum. Ligure 1582.
Thierry, Amedee.   Histoire de Gaulois. 1844.
Tirel, Guillame.   Le Vivandier de Taillevant. 1390.
Ude, Eustace.   The French Cook. 1813.
Vehling, J. D.   Cookery and Dining in Imperial Rome. 1936.
Warner, Rev Richard.   Antiquitatis Culinariae. 1791.
Wilson, C. Anne.   Food and Drink in Britain. 1793.
Wolley, Hannah.   The Accomplish'd Lady's Delight. 1677.
Wynkyn de Worde.   Book of Kervinge. 1508.

Part III
Beauvillier, A de.   L'Art de Cusenier. 1814.
Carrier, Robert.   Great Dishes of the World.
Oliver, Raymond.   The French at Table. 1967.
Young, Mrs.   A few Portsonachan Recipes.

SUPPLIERS ADVERTISEMENTS

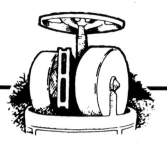

We make
good food
taste especially
delicious

JAMES DALTON
(SEASONING & SPICES) LIMITED

PENNINE RANGE MILLS · STARBECK · HARROGATE HG1 4PY · ENGLAND
TELEPHONE (0423) 885255/8 · TELEX 57903

T·H·E
CAMBRIDGE
H·E·R·B
C O M P A N Y

Suppliers of all things herbal.
Full laboratory facilities.

Units 19 and 20, Dry Drayton Industries
Scotland Road, Dry Drayton, Cambridge CB3 8AT
Telephone: Madingley (0954) 211045/211523
Telex No: 922488 BUREAU G ALB.

THE ESSENCE OF FRAGRANCE AND FLAVOR

J. Manheimer inc.

NATURAL & ARTIFICIAL FLAVORS

MEAT FLAVORS

SAVORY SEASONINGS

bfi

products for the Food Industry

BOVRIL FOOD INGREDIENTS DIVISION. BOVRIL LTD.,
Wellington Road, Burton on Trent. Staffs.
Telephone: (0283) 63781   Telex: 34322

F R BENSON & PARTNERS LIMITED

Suppliers of raw materials and ingredients to the food industry

REPRESENTING IN THE UK

HENNINGSEN FOODS INC.
Spray dried Chicken, Beef, Turkey and Ham Powders
Spray dried Whole Egg, Egg Yolk and Egg White Powders

MELIDA SpA.
Xylose, Xylitol, Fructose, Maltose
Malbit ® Hydrogenated Glucose Syrup

JOUDINAUD & Cie
Roller Dried Fruit and Vegetable Flakes

OTTO WEIMER GmbH
Dehydrated Potato Flakes, Potato Slices, Strips and Dice
Custom made potato based ingredients

SANDERSON AGRUMARIA MERIDIONALE SpA
Fruit Juice Concentrates and Essential Oils
Lemon, Orange, Mandarin and Bergamot

AB CULINAR
Herbs and Spices, Extracts and Essential Oils

Crossroads House, 165 The Parade, High Street, Watford, Herts. WD1 1NJ
Telephone: Watford (0923) 40566   Telex: 22677 Benson G   Cables: Bensonco London W1

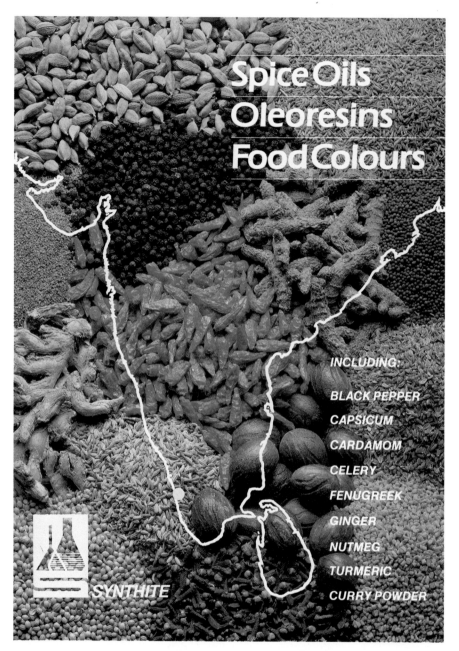

Spice Oils
Oleoresins
Food Colours

INCLUDING:

BLACK PEPPER

CAPSICUM

CARDAMOM

CELERY

FENUGREEK

GINGER

NUTMEG

TURMERIC

CURRY POWDER

SYNTHITE

UGAR CHEMISTRY   METHODS OF ANALYSIS FOR THE CANNING INDUSTRY   SUSTAINABLE FOOD
AL FOOD ADDITIVES – CHARACT   ES INTRODUCTION TO NUTRITION   FOOD
IES OF FOODS AND AGRIC   LE SCIENCE   VITAMIN C – SOME CURR
ALS   POULTRY SCIEN   DEVELOPMENTS IN SOFT DRINKS
ENZYMES FOR FOO   UALITY IN HUMANS: AN IN VITR
METHODS FOR F   ES   FOOD PROCESSING EN
TO FISHERY BY   EAT AND MEAT PRODUCTS
TES   IMPACT   SPITALITY MANAGEMENT
HEESE MAN   DBOOK OF PACKAGING
D HEALTH   CHEMISTRY   FOOD S
NOLOGY A   S, PRODUCTS, APPLICA
S OF ELE   AND ECONOMICS   Q
A OF FO   ACTICAL MEAT CUTT
UAL FOR   AGRICULTURAL PRO
HEMISTR   OCCURENCE OF NITF
ATION   D PATENTS   HYGIEF
Y OF FO   ANNING   YEAST TEC
SIS AND   VEST BIOLOGY AND
HEMISTR   RONI PRODUCTS   FO
HEF   FOO   T   HANDBOOK OF SU
TECHNOLO   IPMENT   SOILS AND C
REEZING OF   ON   BREAD SCIENCE AN
TABLE JUICE   OFFEE TECHNOLOGY
MAKING   BIN   ORN: CULTURE, PR
HYDRATION   LE   E   SE   N BIOLOGY A
TERATURE ON THE   AL THERMO   ANIMAL
RICULTURAL CROPS   AL PRACTICE   A   D THE
LS OF FOOD PROCESS EN   PRINCIPLES   HYGIENI
LIC FOOD SERVICE BEVERAGE   HANDBOOK   EGG SCIENCE & TE
MEAT MARKETING   DRUG-INDUCED NUTRITIONAL DEFICIENCIES   ACIDULANTS FOR FOOD

Creating your unique tastes is our speciality

At Griffith, our taste technologists are unique problem-solvers and innovators. We can effectively create your own distinct taste using your recipe or expanding on a partially developed taste concept. That's our speciality.

But our special expertise lies in making consistency simple. Griffith can quickly give you your own taste efficiently and conveniently, to help you eliminate your costly, time-consuming methods of preparation.

Together we can create your perfect recipe in our test kitchens or at your plant or office. As partners, we'll develop the superior taste, colour, appearance, texture and preparation method you need for your product.

And there's never a compromise on quality at Griffith. Every ingredient is rigidly inspected in our quality control department upon arrival at our plant and again before it's shipped out to you.

Let Griffith create your unique tastes.

Creating them again and again is our special expertise

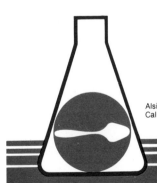

GRIFFITH LABORATORIES

Griffith Laboratories UK Ltd.,
Cotes Park, Somercotes, Derby DE5 4NN.
Telephone: Alfreton (0773) 832171. Telex: 37456.

Also at
Alsip, Illinois USA (Corporate Headquarters) ● Chicago ● Georgia ● New Jersey
California ● Australia ● Belgium ● Canada ● Columbia ● Hong Kong ● Japan
Mexico ● New Zealand ● Panama ● Indonesia ● Spain ● Thailand